ISBN 978-1-5281-1277-2
PIBN 10909043

# 1 MONTH OF
# FREE
# READING

## at
## www.ForgottenBooks.com

By purchasing this book you are eligible for one month membership to ForgottenBooks.com, giving you unlimited access to our entire collection of over 1,000,000 titles via our web site and mobile apps.

To claim your free month visit:
www.forgottenbooks.com/free909043

English
Français
Deutsche
Italiano
Español
Português

# www.forgottenbooks.com

**Mythology** Photography **Fiction**
Fishing Christianity **Art** Cooking
Essays Buddhism Freemasonry
Medicine **Biology** Music **Ancient
Egypt** Evolution Carpentry Physics
Dance Geology **Mathematics** Fitness
Shakespeare **Folklore** Yoga Marketing
**Confidence** Immortality Biographies
Poetry **Psychology** Witchcraft
Electronics Chemistry History **Law**
Accounting **Philosophy** Anthropology
Alchemy Drama Quantum Mechanics
Atheism Sexual Health **Ancient History**
**Entrepreneurship** Languages Sport
Paleontology Needlework Islam
**Metaphysics** Investment Archaeology
Parenting Statistics Criminology
**Motivational**

# - THE -

# Mexico, Peru and Hartford

## TOWN REGISTER

# 1905

COMPILED BY

## MITCHELL AND DAVIS

BRUNSWICK, MAINE:
PUBLISHED BY THE H. E. MITCHELL CO.
1905

# 1770954

Mitchell, Harry Edward, comp.

The Mexico, Peru and Hartford town register, 1905. Comp. by Mitchell and Davis. Brunswick, Me., 1905. O.

# TABLE OF CONTENTS

# Mexico, Peru and Hartford

## TOWN REGISTER

## 1905

✣

## INTRODUCTION.

No more beautiful scenery can be found in the state than presents itself in the rugged landscape of the Oxford Hills, bordering the upper course of the Androscoggin. The surface of the three towns of which we treat, is beautifully varied by hills, lakes, rushing brooks, and the noble river which is to two of the group a bounding line, and for a short distance the dividing line.

This section of Maine was not entered by civilization, except for hunting and trapping, for many decades after the formation of permanent settlements along the coast, and on the lower courses of the great river highways. Gradually, as the native Indian tribes retreated or became weakened by the loss of numbers, the ambitious and progressive white men ventured farther up the river courses or penetrated the great unbroken wilderness; thus gradually but steadily pushing forward the pioneer line, and forcing back-

ward the old order of native ownership of the soil and its
common possession by a race which seemed to delight both
in the liberties of peace, and the vicissitudes of war.

During the last twenty years of the eighteenth century
many townships in Oxford county and the interior of Maine
were granted or sold to men who sought them for the privileges — making for themselves and their families homes
where they should be at peace, and enjoy the liberties so
dearly and heroically bought. Settlement was made in
Hartford soon after the close of the American Revolution,
and in the towns farther north and west very soon following; this was the beginning of a period of remarkable
growth and development, which we shall briefly follow
through the succeeding pages.

# HISTORY OF MEXICO

## HOLMANSTOWN PROPRIETARY.

### PROPRIETORS' RECORD.

Township No. 1, on the north side of the Androscoggin river, was purchased by Col. Jonathan Holman, of the Committee for the Sale of Eastern Lands, for himself and associates, A. D., 1789:—which originated by a subscription, dated at Sutton, Massachusetts, June 26, 1789, as follows:

We, the subscribers, agree to join in the purchase of the (ye) township or piece of land which Dr. Elijah Dix has obtained the refusal of until (tile) the fifth of July next, from the Court's Committee, according to their (its) proposal, dated the 20th inst, wherein they say they will sell to Messrs Holman and Waters, of Sutton, a tract of land lying on the north (side) of the Androscoggin River, and, we hereby agree and engage to pay for the quantity of land we severally and respectively annex (annix) to our names, provided we can have a title to the same, in the tract of land described in said proposals of the Court's Committee according to said proposals.

This tract of land was considered in the subscription for it, as divided into sixty (60) parts or rights, and the subscribers "annex to their names" are, two or more 60ths

(sixtieths). After the first subscription, there were altera-
tions in the quantity of land to some of the subscribers, so
that on (at) the first of Dec., 1787, when there was a general liquidation of all expenses and accounts up to that day,
they stood as follows:

| | | | |
|---|---|---|---|
| Jonathan Holman | 7 | Stephen Stockwell | 1 |
| Asa Waters | 3 | Solomon Holman | 1 |
| Andrew Eliot | 4 | Peter Holman | 1 |
| Asa Goodell | 4 | David Holman | 1 |
| John Holland | 2 | Samuel Bixby | 1 |
| Samuel Small | 1 | Samuel Goodell | 1 |
| Aaron Pierce | 1 | John Goodell | 2 |
| James Taylor | 2 | Joshua Goodell | 2 |
| Nathan Whitmore | 2 | Moody Severy | 1 |
| Gardner Waters | 1 | Elijah Waters | 1 |
| Amos Trask | 1 | Ebenr. Chaplin | 1 |
| Elijah Dix | 13 | Jonas Libby | 1 |
| John Jacobs | 1 | Stephen Prince | 1 |
| Jeremiah Robinson | 2 | John Pierce | 1 |

The following note was added:

"N. B. Although said purchase is said to originate in
the foregoing subscription, yet the matter was negotiated
about 2 years before; and Col. Holman, Dea. Waters, and
Capt. Eliot, spent considerable time and expense, in Aug.
and Sept., 1787, in looking out a township, and picked on
part of the same land now purchased and bespoke (?) it of
the Committee for the sale of Eastern Lands; and as a committee from their Association, in Oct. 1787, went to the
Committee to contract for it, but could not obtain." The

old Association was dissolved and the above entered into.

"Col. Holman went to Boston and contracted for said tract of land July 2nd, 1789, and paid earnest towards it, for himself and others, £391 11s 9d in consolidated notes,— which contract and receipt of said earnest, as also the receipts for £1,340 6s 6d more paid (the) the 17th of Decr. recned as paid at the first of Novr., and £10 6s 3d premium(s) may be seen under hand of Leonard Jarvis, Esqr. which is on file."

At the first proprietors' meeting, held Sept. 13, 1789, Eben Chaplin was chosen moderator and clerk, 9s on a right was raised toward defraying the charges of laying out the township, and Jonathan Holman, Dea. Asa Waters, and Jeremiah Robinson were chosen a committee to perform the work. On Nov. 16, 1789, three rights were sold, one to each, Dr. Dix, Col. Holman and John Pierce.

The plan for the township was made by one Mr. Titcomb, but the lots were laid out by the committee mentioned before, of which we find Col. Holman and Mr. Robinson, in 1790, were directed to "continue to lay out the land in 100 acre lots as far as the land will admit." The township, which then contained the present towns of Dixfield and Mexico, was variously called "Township No. 1," 'Androscoggin Purchase No. 1," and "Holmanstown," until the incorporation of Dixfield, June 21, 1803, the remainder retaining the name of "Holmanstown" until incorporated the town of Mexico fifteen years later.

The meetings of the proprietors were generally held at Sutton, that being the home of the greater number of the

body. Their meetings were continued until Nov. 13, 1809, when, their management being no longer needed, the pro. prietary was brought to an end.

---

# EARLY SETTLEMENT

Who was the first man to enter the town of Mexico to make for himself and family a permanent home, or who was the first to actually locate within the bounds of the present town of Mexico we are now unable to state. Soon after the purchase of the township as shown in the preceding chap. ter, preparations for settling lots were made by the proprie- tors. It is very probable that the first to enter the terri- tory of which we write located near Webb's river, and near the settlers who had taken up lots on the Dixfield side.

Luther Stockwell, son of Stephen Stockwell, one of the proprietors, took up the Stockwell lot, two miles from Dix- field village up the river; he later removed to within a mile of Dixfield. He was the father of Benj. W. one of the most influential men of the succeeding generation in Mexico.

Dea. Joseph Eustis, the father of several celebrated sons, came to this town in 1803 from Rutland, Vt. and located on the lot now occupied by Henry Harlow, one mile from Dixfield village. He was chosen the first town assessor. His son, Charles L., began trading in Dixfield as early as

1805, continuing twenty or more years. About 1831, in connection with a Mr. Clark, of Massachusetts, he purchased the northern half of the town of Eustis and erected a saw and grist mill there, from which the town took its name. Wm Tappan Eustis, at one time an eminent divine in Boston, was later president of the Vermont Central R. R. John M., another son of Joseph, remained on the home place for a while then moved to Dixfield. He was deputy-sheriff, custom-house officer, and filled other positions of honor and trust. Deacon Joseph E. died in Mexico, Dec. 20, 1847.

At Mexico village, or "Corner" as it was formerly called, Isaac Gleason was doubtless the pioneer. He erected his house just back of the site of Henry W. Park's store, and had also a large barn which was entered from two elevations as it stood on an embankment. He had two lots including the entire section upon which the "Corner" village now stands, extending nearly as far as the barber shop below the Goodwin cottages. Some time later Mr. Gleason erected a house nearer the river which stood until a new era was ushered into this locality about fifteen years ago, when activity was begun at Rumford Falls. Members of this family probably have filled more important town offices than has any other family in the history of the town. Elmer H. Gleason, a grandson of Isaac, is now a successful physician in Rumford Falls but resides in this village.

Peter Trask, son of Amos Trask, one of the proprietors and a pioneer at Dixfield, settled on the farm which is now the home of John R. Trask, near the Dixfield line.

Stephen Barnard, the first chosen selectman in town

and one of the most prominent of the early inhabitants, settled one mile from Mexico village on Harlow Hill, on the place now occupied by Elizabeth Richards, a granddaughter. Nathan Knapp was another man to whom this town owes much for the active service rendered during the days of its infancy. He settled on the Harlow Hill road, but later sold his place to Aaron Lufkin, who moved here from Peru; the place is now occupied by the widow of Benj. W. Elliott. Aaron More was another settler on Harlow Hill, the date of his death is one of the very earliest found in the village cemetery.

Capt. Walter P. Carpenter, who was sent a delegate to the constitutional convention at Portland, in 1819, lived in the first house toward Dixfield from Deacon Eustis, on the farm now the home of Frank Leavitt. Captain Carpenter was a man of ability, he was, perhaps, the best educated man in the settlement, and was chosen to fill positions where skill and ingenuity were required.

Moses and John Kimball, brothers, located on the Roxbury road, three-fourths of a mile from Mexico village. Daniel Whitman (mon), the grandfather of Hosea B. Whitman, settled where G. H. Gleason now resides in the village. William Whitman, a brother to Daniel, was another settler here. Harvey Wait married Lucy, a daughter of Dea. Joseph Eustis, and built up a home on the place now known as the Isaac Bradeen place. Benj. Edmonds, who was chosen collector to succeed Daniel Porter, lived on the last farm in Mexico on the west side of Swift river.

Zebediah Mitchell who lived near the bank of Swift river,

3½ miles above the village, near Frye postoffice, was one of the earliest in this locality. James Mitchell, probably no connection of the first mentioned, settled in what became known as the "Back Kingdom," where he raised a large family, but this family is now nearly extinct in Mexico. Daniel Porter, John and Jacob Lufkin, Jedediah Farnum and several others were among the men who came to this town when its surface was an unbroken forest, except for here and there the narrow clearing of a pioneer who had entered the wilderness a little in advance of his neighbor.

Of the first traders and professional men we would mention Curtis P. Howe as probably the earliest to open a store for the sale of codfish, molasses and New England rum, the three necessary, or staple articles sought at the early "grocery." Henry W. Park, to whom we are indebted for much of the data given in this account, came to this village from Dixfield about 1845 since which time he has been one of the most prominent citizens, having been in trade much of that time, filling the office of selectman during the early years of the Civil war, enlisting volunteers and recruits for the service, and in other ways serving the locality.

Dr. Walker, whose residence occupied the site of Mr. Park's house, was probably the first educated physician. Dr. Arad Farwell, who was also prominent in town affairs, was another early practitioner. Dr. Tracy was located here before the breaking out of the war. Dr. Victor M. Abbott was a successful and prominent man in his profession. Dr. H. J. Binford and Dr. H. O. Hanlon are now in practice here.

Judge Chas. W. Walton, of the Supreme Court of the State, was the first to open a law office in Mexico, and in fact, about the only member of the bar who has opened an office here except N. G. Foster at Ridlonville. John R. Trask, who lives in Mexico, has an office in Dixfield.

Until fifteen years ago this town was, like many other towns of the state at the present time, devoted chiefly to her own interests, and connected in no way with the outside world. With the development of the water power at Rumford Falls and the remarkable growth of that village, Mexico has shared in its prosperity. Many new residences have been erected here during the past ten years, but its local industries have not become greatly multiplied. The population of the town in 1900 was but 816; it is now estimated at over 2000, showing a growth equalled only by the village of which this is virtually a part.

## INCORPORATION

What was the government of "Holmanstown Plantation" after the incorporation of Dixfield, in 1803, until the incorporation of the town of Mexico, Feb. 13, 1818, we find no record. The final meeting of the proprietors seems to have been held in 1809, as we have shown earlier, but before the proprietary was dissolved it had little power over actual,

legal settlers.  Since the Act of Incorporation calls it "Hol-manstown Plantation" we conclude that there had for a few years existed a plantation organization in the township.

## ACT OF INCORPORATION

Commonwealth of Massachusetts.  In the year of our Lord one thousand eight hundred and eighteen.  An act to establish the town of Mexico in the county of Oxford.

Sec. 1.  Be it enacted by the Senate and House of Representatives in General Court assembled and by the authority of the same, That the plantation heretofore called Holmanstown on the north side of Great Androscoggin river, in the County of Oxford, as contained within the following described boundaries, be and the same is hereby incorporated and established as a town by the name of Mexico, viz.: Eastwardly by Webb's river (the present bounds between Dixfield and said Holmanstown) Southerly by the river Great Amariscoggin, Westerly by the town of Rumford, Northerly by the townships or plantations numbered four and seven; and the inhabitants of the said town of Mexico are hereby vested with all the powers and privileges and shall be also subject to all the duties and requisitions of other corporate towns according to the constitution and laws of this commonwealth.

Sec. 2.  Be it further enacted, That any Justice of the peace for the County of Oxford, upon application therefor is hereby empowered to issue a warrant, directed to a freeholder inhabitant of the said town of Mexico requiring him to notify and warn the inhabitants thereof to meet at such

convenient time and place as shall be appointed in the said warrant for the choice of such officers as towns are by law empowered and required to choose at their annual meetings.

In the House of Representatives Feby. 12th, 1818.
This bill having had three several readings passed to be enacted.

TIMOTHY BIGELOW, *Speaker.*

In Senate February 13th, 1818.
This bill having had two several readings passed to be enacted.

JOHN PHILLIPS, *President.*

February 13th, 1818.
Approved.

J. BROOKS, *Governor.*

A warrant calling the first town meeting of the freeholders of Mexico was issued by Francis Keyes, Esq., and directed to Nathan Knapp. The meeting was called at the dwelling house of Isaac Gleason, on Monday, March 20th, 1818, at which time and place the following town officers were balloted for and elected:

Joseph Eustis, moderator; Nathan Knapp, town clerk; Stephen Barnard, Isaac Gleason and Daniel Whitman, selectmen; Joseph Eustis, Harvey Wait and John Lufkin, assessors; Moses Kimball, town treasurer. Other necessary officers were chosen by hand vote, among the number being Aaron More and Wm. Whitmon, tythingmen.

On the sixth of April the freeholders of this new municipality cast their vote for a Governor and Lieutenant Gov-

ernor of Massachusetts, and for a Senator from their district. For Governor, ten (presumably all that were qualified to vote) cast votes, Hon. Benj. W. Crowningshield receiving eight, and Hon. John Brooks, two.

We find that on August 1, 1818, Benj. Edmonds was chosen collector in place of Daniel Porter, "absconded." Mr. Porter however could not have gone far on the "funds" in his possession, and we are told that he returned soon after.

The final vote of this town on the question of separating the District of Maine from Massachusetts and establishing it a free and independent state was cast July 26, 1819, when the vote was unanimous in favor of separation, 12 votes cast. Walter P. Carpenter was chosen a delegate to represent the town in the Constitutional Convention at Portland, which met soon after this to form the Constitution for the new State.

# TOWN OFFICIALS

### CLERKS, SINCE 1850

P. S. Wilson, 1850; John Kelsey, 1851-52; P. S. Wilson, 1853; John Kelsey, 1854; Chas. W. Walton, 1855; John Holland, 1856-57; Arad Farwell, 1858; John Holland, 1859; Arad Farwell, 1860-61; David O. Gleason, 1862-66;

MPH2

C. T. Gleason, 1867-70; David O. Gleason, 1871-83; Lamont
C. Willoughby, 1884; L. H. Harlow, 1885-86; Lewis H.
Reed, 1887-90; L. H. Harlow, 1891-93; W. C. Stevens,
1894-95; John L. Howard, 1896-1900; A. D. Virgin,
1901-05.

### TOWN TREASURERS

Lewis Reed, 1850-52; Barnard L. Marble, 1853; Aaron
Lufkin, 1854; Henry F. Durgin, 1855; Lewis Reed, 1856;
Benj. W. Stockwell, 1857; A. J. Mitchell, 1858; B. W. Stockwell, 1859; Benj. Thomas, 1860; P. M. Edmonds, 1861;
David F. Brown, 1862; Dura Bradford, 1863-66; J. H. Gleason, 1867-68, Benj. W. Stockwell, 1869; H. W. Park,
1870-93; H. J. Binford, 1894-1902; Hosea B. Whitman,
1904-05.

### SELECTMEN

1850—Peter Trask, Wm. H. Whitman, Benj. Edmonds
Jr.

1851—Peter Trask, Wm. H. Whitman, Jos. R. Hall.
1852—John Kelsey, John M. Eustis, Thos. Harlow.
1853—John Kelsey, Thos. Harlow, A. H. Mitchell.
1854—I. N. Stanley, Samuel Morrill, Lewis Reed.
1855—I. N. Stanley, C. P. Howe, Chas. W. Walton.
1856-7—Lewis Reed, Jona. Mitchell, H. L. Austin.
1858—I. N. Stanley, Levi Hayes, Benj. Edmonds Jr.
1859—Jona. Mitchell, B. W. Stockwell, Chas. A. Scott.
1860—C. A. Scott, H. F. Durgin, S. C. Gleason.
1861—C. A. Scott, H. L. Austin, John Larrabee.

1862-4—John Larrabee, Henry W. Park, B. W. Stock-well.

1865—John Larrabee, B. W. Stockwell, P. M. Edmonds.

1866—Peter Trask, P. M. Edmonds, D. O. Gleason.

1867—P. M. Edmonds, D. O. Gleason, Wm. M. Hall.

1868—D. O. Gleason, B. W. Stockwell, J. Larrabee.

1869—Wm. Woodbury, J. Larrabee, Jarvis W. Richards.

1870—B. W. Stockwell, J. W. Richards, J. H. Gleason.

1871—J. W. Richards, J. Larrabee, Sewell Goff.

1872—Sewell Goff, O. F. Trask, B. W. Elliott.

1873-74—Sewell Goff, O. F. Trask, John F. Stanley.

1875-76—J. F. Stanley, O. F. Trask, F. G. Parsons.

1877—John F. Stanley, O. F. Trask, Geo. H. Gleason.

1878—O. F. Trask, G. H. Gleason, B. W. Elliott.

1879-81—O. F. Trask, G. H. Gleason, Jarvis W. Richards.

1882-83—O. F. Trask, Erastus Hayes, Sewell Goff.

1884—O. F. Trask, E. Hayes, Stilman A. Reed.

1885-86—S. A. Reed, Geo. W. Roberts, F. C. Richards.

1887-88—S. A. Reed, Scott O. Door, Hiram T. Richards.

1889—H. T. Richards, G. H. Gleason, R. L. Taylor.

1890—G. H. Gleason, R. L. Taylor, Dan'l G. Frost.

1891—R. L. Taylor, D. G. Frost, E. R. Harrington.

1892—D. G. Frost, E. R. Harrington, H. T. Richards.

1893—E. R. Harrington, H. T. Richards, G. H. Gleason.

1894—R. L. Taylor, C. M. Holland, H. B. Whitman.

1895—R. L. Taylor, H. B. Whitman, W. C. Stephens.

1896—H. B. Whitman, R. L. Taylor, Milo Mitchell.

1897—H. B. Whitman, R. L. Taylor, F. Kidder.

1898—H. B. Whitman, R. L. Taylor, D. L. Hathorn.
1899—H. B. Whitman, R. L. Taylor, Jas. M. Doyen.
1900—H. B. Whitman, Jas. M. Doyen, J. R. Austin.
1901-02—J. M. Doyen, J. R. Austin, S. A. Reed.
1903—J. R. Austin, S. A. Reed, David O. Gleason.
1904—S. A. Reed, H. T. Richards, J. L. Howard.
1905—H. L. Richards, H. A. LeBarron, B. W. Goodwin.

## INDUSTRIAL ACCOUNT.

The earliest manufacturing in the town of Mexico was
not an industry peculiar to that town but one common to
most of the towns of the state. We have great respect for
our fathers who erected their first rude cabins of unsawed
and unhewn logs, and in which they made their first homes.
We should remember, however, that these were not their
permanent homes, but were erected to serve only until sufficient footing could be secured to erect more substantial
homes, and the necessary lumber be prepared in the community. The latter need demanded the erection of saw mills,
although the house frames were generally hewed by hand.
The early mills were located on the natural water privileges
on the larger brooks and small rivers. In testimony of the
substantial homes erected during the years following the
first few years of preparation, we now have, standing gen-

erally on hill-tops or high ground, many of the two-story, square houses which were heated by large open fire-places, one of which was generally provided for each room.

The first mill constructed in Mexico, so far as H. W. Park, the local historian, is able to determine, was built on Mitchell Brook, near the Roxbury line. This mill was run by an over-shot wheel and did good service for some years, but is now obliterated.

Another early mill was erected by Adam Knight on the west bank of Webb's river, about a mile above Dixfield village. This mill was later operated by Chas. L. Eustis, Humphrey Eaton and John M. Eustis.

On the site of the toothpick mill in Mexico, near Dixfield village, was at one time an axe manufactory, fitted up with trip-hammers, and occupied by Edmunds & Gardner, this occupied the ground floor while above was Dillingham & Burnham's cabinet shop. This building was burned and a new one erected by Hosea Austin and Stockbridge Eaton, who used it for manufacturing birch boxes of all kinds. The mill was later transformed into a toothpick factory.

The toothpick factory which is now operated as the estate of Charles Forster, O. H. Hersey, trustee, is located on the Mexico side of Webb's river, but is practically a Dixfield industry. The mill which occupied this site for many years, and which had been occupied for this business for some time, was burned January 5, 1904. It was immediately rebuilt, and operations were begun in the new mill August 15, 1904. One hundred hands, about half of whom are women, are employed here. One hundred cases, each containing one

hundred boxes of 1800 picks, are manufactured per day.

At the other extremity of the town, near the present Hale postoffice, was an early saw and grist mill. This was operated by Alvin Wesley and Blanchard Kimball, for a long period of years. During the "Flood of 1869," which is well remembered by some of our readers, everything that could be swept away was carried off and the place left looking almost as though it had never been the site of an active business industry. The site was soon purchased by F. C. Richards & Son, who erected a long and short lumber mill. They sold to Wm. Wallace Mason some years ago. A good business, including the manufacturing of novelties, is now carried on here by Mason Bros.

After selling the above mill F. C. Richards & Son built a steam mill two miles below the village. This is now operated by the son, Allen W. Richards, who manufactures long and short lumber, and spool stock.

About 1854 Chas. A. Scott erected a lumber mill, driven by an overshot wheel, on Austin Brook, in the "Back Kingdom." M. E. Tucker formerly erected and operated a steam mill, near the toll bridge, for manufacturing novelties and turning wooden goods. During the 70's O. P. Tucker and Frank Parsons erected a steam mill for manufacturing long lumber and axe-handle blocks, on the site of the present town house.

There may have been other mills in the town before the primeval forest was turned to lumber, but some of the logs were formerly floated down the river to other centers.

# MILITARY MATTERS.

The military record of the town of Mexico is one of which her citizens are justly proud. The first national war after the settlement of the town was the second struggle with Great Britain for national freedom. Ebenezer Dorr and Harry Mitchell fought in the American Army during this war. Mr. Mitchell again joined the military ranks during the Aroostook War, and marched to Houlton. When marching through the streets of that town it is said that he was recognized by General Winfield Scott, with whom he fought in 1812. Joshua T. Hall was commissioned a captain in the Aroostook forces.

### CIVIL WAR.

The service performed by the soldiers who served their country during the great civil struggle proved the military powers of a devoted people. We give below a list of the men credited to the town as recorded on the State Adjutant General's reports for the years 1861-1865. Of the number, Dr. Tracy was assistant surgeon, and Lieut. John A. Kidder served in the 1st, 23d, and 29th regiments. Henry W. Park did military duty in the city of Washington, being mustered into service for guard duty. Mr. Park was also an enlisting officer for the section.

Lorenzo Conant, Charles A. Eastman, Arthur S. Mitchell, Edwin D. Waite, Aaron S. Larrabee, Henry H. Mitchell, John O. Kidder, Wm. W. Foss, Charles H. Austin, Azro R. Durgin, Geo. C. Eastman, Van R. Eastman, Elbridge G. Hall, Frank G. Parsons, Levi Hayes, Harrison F. Whitman, Charles F. Walker, Charles M. Downs, Alfred B. Putnam, Wyman Dorrington, John O. Kidder, George Dolly, Thomas Holmes, Roscoe E. Harlow, Arthur S. Mitchell, Charles N. Downes, Joseph A. Parsons, Daniel A. Whitman, James K. P. Simpson, Joel M. Gleason, Daniel E. Durgin, Cyrus Gammon, Charles Walker, David J. Parsons, Sanford M. Reed, Theodore S. Downes, Edw. E. Hayes, Erastus Hayes, Virgil L. Pierce, Aaron S. Larrabee, Jos. E. Lovejoy, Edwin D. Waite, Virgil Dillingham, Neri D. B. Durgin, Gleason J Hayes, Lesmore Kidder, Chas. Walker, Orlando H. Eastman, Martin V. Caston, Ladoc G. Eastman, Anjer F. Mitchell, Gardiner F. Randlett, Andrew S. Ayer, Lorenzo Conant, Joel M. Babb, Josiah Smith, Wm. H. Wiley, Rosalve A. York, Wm. McKeen.

# CHURCH AFFAIRS

So far as we have learned, the early religious services attended by the residents of the town of Mexico were held either at Rumford, just across the Androscoggin, or at Dixfield village, just across Webb's river. The earliest society in town for the promotion of religious worship of which we have obtained account, was the Union Church Society, formed January 25th, 1890, when a number of citizens who had contributed toward the erection of a hall over the town hall, then being built, became organized for its management. A word should be said of the important part taken by the Ladies' Sewing Circle, which gave the first few hundred dollars toward the erection of the hall. It was dedicated to the use of all orthodox religious societies. The hall was first occupied by the Methodists, who maintained more or less regular preaching for several months. It was then occupied by the Free Baptists, Methodists and Congregationalists successively, the latter occupying it about eighteen months before dedicating their new house of worship on Main street. After the completion of this church edifice the hall was no longer needed for religious worship and was sold to the Junior Order of American Mechanics, by which order, and by the Patrons of Husbandry, it is now used. Formerly the U. O. G. C. and the A. O. U. W. held their meetings here.

The Congregational Church Society was organized October 25, 1902, in the Union Hall. The next year the beauti-

ful new church was begun, and was dedicated to the worship
of God in June, 1904, costing about $8,000. At the time of
organization the society numbered but 22 members. Since
that time, 64 others have united with them, and the work of
the church has been greatly increased. Rev. Chas. L. Par-
ker was the first pastor, remaining until quite recently.
Rev. J. G. Fisher is the newly installed pastor. The church
sees before it a large field and bright prospects of success
and usefulness in its all-important work of winning souls for
God.

## SCHOOL ITEMS.

Hardly had the town of Mexico been launched on its
career as an organized body when steps were made toward
the formation of school districts, and the establishment of
systematic education. About two months after the passing
of the Incorporation Act the voters raised the sum of $60
for this purpose, and had the town divided into districts as
follows: The sixth, seventh, and eighth ranges of the town
formed the "North District," and the dividing line between
the "Eastern" and "Western" districts extended from the
Androscoggin river beginning between lots, seven and eight
in range one. "School wards" were chosen; viz: Zebediah
Mitchell warden of the North district, Nathan Knapp, of
the Western district, and Joseph Eustis of the Eastern district.

On Dec. 29, 1818, the selectmen of this town appointed a

committee to petition the legislature, with Dixfield, for per-
mission to sell ministerial and school lands which were lo-
located within the townships. These public lands which were
laid out and given by the proprietors of "Township No. 1,"
were, according to the act incorporating the town of Dixfield, in 1813, divided between that town and what became
the town of Mexico, in proportion to their several areas.
From the sale of the school lands a sufficient sum was
realized by the town to establish a fund of some value.

The improvement and development of the schools of
this town has been similar to that of most country towns
of the state during the same period. The voters have been
liberal in their appropriations for educational support, and
the advancement made has been such as to show the steady
development of a system introducing modern methods of
instruction, improved text books and a more efficient corps
of teachers.

The first free High school was held in what is now known
as the "Old School-house" in the village. The present modern High school building was erected in 1894, and is the
home of both the High and Grammar schools. The building contains six large rooms, is provided with modern improvements and is centrally located for the students of the
village section where is a very large percent of the population. Under Fred A. Robinson, with Helena O. Park, assistant, a High school course was laid out. This has been
enlarged and improved by succeeding instructors. There is
now a regular four years course of instruction which pre-
pares its students for college work, or is intended to round

out a practical education for those who are unable to enter
institutions of higher educational advantages.  The list of
principals who have been employed in the High school, following Mr. Robinson, is Rufus H. Douglass, Vena L. Richards, George Miner, G. H. D. L'Amoureux, Irving R.
Hawkes, and the present principal, J. W. Taylor who has
remained here two years.

A new school building was completed last year, to be occupied by the Primary and Intermediate grades of the village schools.  The building was erected at a cost of $5,000.
The houses throughout the rural section of the town are
either new or in very good repair, and the instruction given
is generally such as to give general satisfaction where it is
impossible for the scholars to enter the graded schools.

## PATRONS OF HUSBANDRY.

Swift River Grange, Number 107, was reorganized May
10, 1904, the charter having been given an earlier organization here about 30 years ago.  The reorganized Grange
began with about twenty-five members, which number has
now increased to eighty-eight.  Ira T. Wing was the first
Master, and has continued the second year.  The other principal officers for the year 1905 are O. P. Smith, Overseer;
R. L. Taylor Jr., Lec.; Mrs. Thos. L. Weeks, Chap.; Geo. H.
Gleason, Treas.; and Grace E. Park, Sec.  The regular meetings are held in the American Mechanics Hall, on Main
street.

# HISTORY OF PERU

## EARLY SETTLEMENT

The nucleus of the town of Peru was a grant of two miles square, made by Massachusetts, to Merrill Knight, Daniel Lunt, William Brackett, and a Mr. Bradish of Falmouth. Subsequently the remainder of the township was granted or sold in tracts to E. Fox Lunt, Capt. Wm. Thompson, and a Mr. Peck. The first grant, and that later granted to Mr. Lunt well known as "Lunt's Upper and Lower Tracts," the other grants were known by the names of their grantees.

Merrill Knight is accorded the honor of having been the earliest to make a permanent home within the bounds of what is now Peru. He came from Falmouth, now Portland, in 1793, proceeding with his family through an unbroken forest to the banks of the Androscoggin. He erected a rude cabin northwest of Stony Brook, about one-half mile from the present Centre village, on the place now occupied by Mr. Guptil. It is said just as he was moving into the cabin from a hospitable neighbor's about two miles distant, when arriving with the last load of goods the cabin was discovered to be on fire and was soon in ashes. Disheartened Mr. Knight would have returned to Falmouth but the neighbor down the river again took his family to his own cabin where

they remained until he could rebuild.

William Walker, who afterwards became the first plantation treasurer and for many years a leading spirit in the settlement, is said to have been the next settler, coming as early as 1802. He located where Henry Robinson now lives. Hezekiah, his son, remained on the home place. He was plantation and town clerk for a long term of years, and seems to have been a man of some wealth for in 1819 the town voted $3.00 to pay him interest for money loaned to pay the county tax. Wm. Walker, Jr. opened the first hotel in Peru in 1831, in the house now occupied by his son, Wm. II. Walker, one mile northwest from the Center. Here was also opened the earliest postoffice in town, kept in the hotel, and receiving mails weekly from Dixfield. George Walker, a brother to Wm. Sr., arrived in town soon after 1802 and settled the farm now occupied by D. W. Knight. Daniel Lunt, probably the son of the grantee, was among the earliest arrivals here. He cleared the farm on a part of which Manderville Hall now lives. His brother, James, came about the same time.

Osborn Trask and Brady Bailey, both of Falmouth, soon followed, the latter's lot being two and one-half miles from the Center, in what became known as the "Bailey Neighborhood" now the name is nearly extinct in town. Wm. Brackett, one of the proprietors of the first grant, or a son of the same name, located on the river road, above Peru Center. Jabez Delano located not far from Brady Bailey. Joshua Knox was an early settler in the southwestern part of the town; he had a large family, many of

his sons settling around him, and the locality became known as the "Knox Neighborhood." Among his sons were Samuel, Seth, Eben and Obed.

Burgess Hill, in West Peru, was the home of several families of that name who came very early in the history of the town. Levi Ludden occupied the farm on which is now located West Peru and Dixfield railroal depot. James H. Withington, another prominent man in the early town, settled farther up the river on a farm within the territory set off to Rumford in 1895.

In the eastern part of the town Benjamin Wormell was one of the earliest to locate. It was in his house that the early Baptist church was organized, in 1818. Robinson Turner, an early mill operator, and Francis Wait both set-tled in this part of the town, Mr. Wait settling the place now occupied by Hiram E. Stillman. Wm. Kyle was living where Henry Chase now resides in March 1812.

Edsell Grover, an early collector in the plantation, Amos Knight, John Holland, Wm. Millett, David Dore, and Daniel Deshon were all settled here and filled office in the plantation prior to 1820. This was a prosperous period in the history of the locality, the land was new and fertile and the farmers were not competing with the products of exten-sive Western fields where large quantities could be produced at much less cost than in this broken section. New roads were being laid out each year, school and social privileges annually improved, and the general condition of affairs such as to make glad the hearts of the sturdy pioneers who had pressed forward to a land unknown, far from family and

friends, to make for themselves and for their posterity homes that should give them liberty, prosperity and happiness, even if bought by many and long days of toil.

## PLANTATION NUMBER ONE

The earliest records of the town of Peru begin with the organization of the township as Plantation No. 1, on March 23, 1812, when the scattering inhabitants assembled in answer to a warrant issued by Henry Rust, Esq., county treasurer of Oxford county. John Holland, Esq., was chosen moderator; Hezekiah Walker, plantation clerk, which office he held until the incorporation of the town of Peru, and filled the office of town clerk until March 9, 1829. Amos Knight, James Lunt, and William Kyle were chosen assessors. Adam Knight bid off the collection of taxes 10 cents on a dollar; evidently not an easy matter.

On April 6th, 1812, the second plantation meeting was called, place not designated in the records, but for the purpose of casting votes for governor for the Commonwealth of Massachusetts, and senators for this District. After choosing Merrill Knight, moderator, twenty votes were cast for Elbridge Gerry for governor, and the same number for William King, lieutenant governor. The number of votes cast for senators were the same for each, the following three men

being voted for: Hon. Eleazer W. Ripley, Jonathan Page and Ebenezer Poor.

The second annual election of Plantation officers was conducted similar to the first. Adam Knight seems not to have found the collection of taxes any easier than he expected for we find he was given 12% for collection the second year. William Walker was the chosen treasurer, which is ths earliest election to this office that we find, and as no sums had been appropriated it is probable that neither a collector nor a treasurer was needed the first year.

A sum of $50 was then appropriated for the support of schools, and school districts laid out as follows: "The lower district to extend from the Jay (now Canton) line up to Daniel Lunt's house, and the upper district to extend from Daniel Lunt's house to the Rumford line, the western district to extend from Amos Knight's to the Sumner line.

In December, 1813, the inhabitants displayed a remarkable spirit of progress and ambition, several new roads were voted to be laid out, and a vote was made "to have a man's school at Mr. Merrill Knight's two months this winter and two months next summer in the eastern and western districts." Amos King, Hezekiah Walker and Robinson Turner were chosen a school committee. Doubtless the schools of this period required a stern master, who was able to administer the birch rod, as well as instruct his pupils in Arithmetic, reading and spelling.

In 1815, the sum of $500 was raised for highways, but nothing for schools, $30 however, seems to have been used for this purpose, it may have been a surplus left from the

$50 voted for schools the preceding year.

The number of voters increased slowly, yet the community was increasing in population and improvements, and the settlers began to think of incorporation, and on May 20th, 1816, a vote was taken, but they were not ready to meet the expense of town government. At this time the school districts were united, and $150 raised to erect a suitable school house near the center of the town. After the completion of this house, in 1817, it was used instead of Mr. Knight's house, for holding the plantation meetings.

In July, 1819, this town cast 29 votes in favor of separating Maine from Massachusetts and establishing a separate State, none were against the measure. On April 3, 1820, 40 votes were thrown for Hon. Wm. King for the first governor of the new State.

Steps toward incorporation were now being made. In November, 1820, the assessors of the Plantation were instructed to see who were "in the town at the time of incoration." A complete list of the families then taken is recorded in the Plantation records, with the names of each, from which we have taken the following list.

This closes the records of PLANTATION NUMBER ONE, which records were later made valid by special act of Legislature, they having been defectively recorded.

## LIST OF INHABITANTS

Of Peru at time of Incorporation, Feb. 5, 1821.

Numbers given in parentheses are not sons or daughters but male or female members of the family.

| Head of family | wife | sons | daugh. |
|---|---|---|---|
| Austin, Henry | Hannah | 1 | 2 |
| Adkins, David | Margery | 3 | 3 |
| Adkins, Owen | Mary | 0 | 1 |
| Burges, Samuel | Hannah | 0 | 0 |
| Burges, Ebenezer | Sele | 2 | 0 |
| Burges, Seth | Virtue | 4 | 5 |
| Burges, Obediah | Melinda | 0 | 1 |
| Bailey, Brady | Nancy | 1 | 0 |
| Bailey, Samuel | Charlotte | 0 | 0 |
| Barton, Daniel | Eunice | 1 | 0 |
| Brock, William | | | |
| Brackett, William | Betty | 3 | 1 |
| Babb, George | Miriam | 0 | 1 |
| Curtis, Josiah | Ellenor | (1 servant boy) | |
| Cobb, Abial | Eunice | 2 | 1 |
| Dennet, Moses | Margaret | 1 | 0 |
| Doer, David | Sarah | 0 | 0 |
| Doer, Nathaniel | Mary | 0 | 0 |
| Dileno, Jabez | Grace | 2 | 3 |
| Dileno, Abial | Sarah | 0 | 2 |
| Dileno, John | Mahitable | 1 | 0 |

| | | | |
|---|---|---|---|
| Ellis, John | | | |
| Furnold, Edmond | Betsy | 1 | 0 |
| Fobes, Benjamin | Bethiah | 2 | 5 |
| Freeman, Sampson | Catherine | 1 | 3 |
| Gammond, Stephen | | | |
| Gilcrease, John | Mary | 2 | 0 |
| Grover, Jedediah | Elizabeth | 1 | 2 |
| Hammond, Sylvanus | Betsey | (1) | 4 |
| Hammond, Paul | | | |
| Hammond, Paul Jr | —— | 1 | (1)1 |
| Hall, Jeremiah | | | |
| Hall, Jonathan | | | |
| Hall, Jefferson | | | |
| Hopkins, Oliver | Nancy | 3 | 1 |
| Hoit, David | Sarah | | |
| Knight, John | Nancy | 4 | 0 |
| Knight, Amos | Lucy | 3 | 3 |
| Knight, Going | Betsy | 1 | 2 |
| Knight, Adam | Betsy | 2 | 1 |
| Knight, Henry | Thursy | 2 | 0 |
| Knight, Merril | Rachel | 0 | 2 |
| Knight, Samuel | Olive | 3 | 4 |
| Lunt, Daniel | Roda | 2 | 2 |
| Lunt, James | Mercy | (1) | 4 |
| Lunt, Francis | Lydia | 3 | 0 |
| Lunt, George | | | |
| Jenna, Joseph | Betsy | 2 | 0 |
| Kyle, William | Rebecca | 1 | 2 |
| Kyle, Amos | Charity | 1 | 2 |

| | | | |
|---|---|---|---|
| Knox, Joshua | Polly | (1)2 | (1) |
| Hodsden, John | Eliza | | |
| Ludden, Levi | Phebe | (1)2 | (1)2 |
| Poland, John | Fear | 1 | 1 |
| Poland, Dorcas (mother of John) | | | |
| Lufkin, Benj | Mahitable | 2 | 2 |
| Millet, William | Betsy | 3 | 1 |
| Roberts, Seth | Miriam | 2 | 1 |
| Swift, Nathaniel | Polly | 3 | 3 |
| Thomas, Elijah | | | |
| Thurston, True | Priscilla | 6 | 1 |
| Turner, Robinson | Lillie | 1 | 3 |
| Walker, William | Sibyl | 1 | 1 |
| Walker, Hezekiah | Dorcas | 0 | 0 |
| Walker, George | Melinda | 0 | 1 |
| Walker, Wm Jr | Mercy | 2 | 1 |
| Walker, Nathan | Fanny | 0 | 0 |
| Wormell, Benj | Anna | 4 | 0 |
| Withington, James | Sarah | 3 | 2 |
| Wait, Francis | Dorcas | 3 | 3 |
| Wing, Stephen | Patty | 3 | 3 |
| Hutchins, Joseph | Sarah | 4 | 3 |

Smith, Judith ⎫
Smith, A^xey ⎭ daughters of Amos L. Smith

A total of 341 inhabitants.

# ACT OF INCORPORATION

## STATE OF MAINE.

In the year of our Lord one thousand eight hundred and twenty one.—

An act to establish the town of Peru in the County of Oxford.—

Section 1. Be it enacted by the Senate and House of Representatives in Legislature assembled: That the Plantation heretofore called Number one, in the County of Oxford, as contained within the following described bounds, be and hereby is, with the inhabitants thereon, established as a town by the name of PERU and bounded as follows, to wit; West by the town of Rumford and Plantation number two, South by the town of Sumner, East by the town of Hartford and Jay (now Canton), and North by the Androscoggin River. And the said town of PERU is hereby vested with all the corporate powers and privileges and shall be subject to all the duties and requisitions of other corporate Towns, according to the Constitution and Laws of this State.

Section 2. Be it further enacted that Stephen Barnard Esq. of Mexico in said County, upon application therefor is hereby empowered to issue a warrant directed to a freeholder inhabitant of said town of PERU, requiring him to notify and warn the inhabitants of said town to meet at such convenient time and place as shall be appointed in said warrant, for the choice of such officers as towns are by law

empowered and required to choose at their annual town meetings.

Approved by
Governor WILLIAM KING
February 5th, 1821.

Esq. Barnard issued his warrant to Wm. Brackett, calling the meeting April 4, 1821, at the School House. The following officers were selected to man this new government; Amos Knight, moderator of the meeting. Hezekiah Walker continued clerk; James Lunt, Josiah Curtis and Amos Knight, were chosen selectmen and assessors; Wm. Walker Jr., town treasurer; Wm. Brackett, collector (@4%) and constable; and all other necessary town officers, including Geo. Walker, James H. Withington and Abial Dilano, tythingmen.

At the second town meeting, April 16, 1821, Wm. Brackett was chosen town agent, $700 raised for repair of highways; $150 for support of schools, and a like sum to defray town charges.

In answer to an article in the town warrant the town voted to settle Enoch Jaques, as a town minister, and that he should have one half the Minister lands in the town and the use of all the Ministerial lands while he should continue to preach in town.

Soon after, on account of the scarcity of specie, a vote was made that town taxes might be paid in corn or grain. Six school districts were laid out in the fall of 1821, by James Lunt, Josiah Curtis, Edsell Grover and Nathan

Walker,—committee.

For many years the bounds of Peru remained unchang-
ed until Feb. 21, 1895, when that part of Peru west of a
line drawn along the southeasterly lines of lots No. 29, 28,
27, 26, and 25, from Androscoggin river, were sold to Rumford for $2,000, at the same time Franklin Plantation (for-
merly plantation Number 2) was divided and a portion an-
nexed to Peru.

Franklin Plantation was composed of Buxton, Milton
Academy and Bartlett Grants, and was about 5 miles long
and half as wide. The first clearing was made in 1816, and
the first settlement in 1820. General settlement was made
about ten years later, and the plantation organized in 1841.
The population in 1870 was 178, and in 1880, 159.

## TOWN   OFFICIALS

### CLERKS.

We have endeavored to compile a complete list of the
clerks, treasurers and selectmen since 1850 but one of the
books of the Town Clerk with records from 1850 to 1875 is
not to be found, hence our omission for those years. W. S.
Walker, 1875-'79; Winslow Walker, 1880-'84; O. C. Hopkins, 1885-'91; S. F. Robinson, 1892-'95; O. C. Hopkins,
1886; S. F. Robinson, 1897-1901; W. S. Arnold, 1902-'05.

## TREASURERS.

Winslow Walker, 1875; W. S. Walker, 1876-'79; Edwin Babb, 1881; Wm. H. Walker, 1882; Henry Robinson, 1883-'87; A. A. Babb, 1888; Fred O. Walker, 1889; Howard Turner, 1890-'92; D. W. Walker, 1893; W. S. Walker, 1894-'99; H. Robinson, 1905.

## SELECTMEN.

1875—Josiah Hall, Benj. Lovejoy, D. F. Bishop.
1876—Benj. Lovejoy, D. H. Bishop, H. S. McIntire.
1877—D. F. Bishop, H. F. McIntire, Noah Hall.
1878—H. S. McIntire, Noah Hall, Henry Rowe.
1879—Noah Hall, Henry Rowe, J. Hall.
1880—Henry Rowe, J. Hall, H. S. McIntire.
1881—J. Hall, H. S. McIntire, John Knight.
1882—H. S. McIntire, Hollis Turner, G. O. Hussey.
1883—H. S. McIntire, G. O. Hussey, Winslow Walker.
1884—W. S. Walker, H. Turner, W. Walker.
1885—W. S. Walker, Wm. Woodsum, D. W. Goding.
1886—W. S. Walker, D. W. Goding, J. W. Gowell.
1887—D. W. Goding, J. W. Gowell, T. H. Burgess.
1888-'89—J. W. Gowell, D. W. Goding, H. R. Robinson.
1890—D. W. Goding, H. R. Robinson, J. W. Gowell.
1891—H. R. Robinson, J. W. Gowell, O. C. Hopkins.
1892—J. W. Gowell, O. C. Hopkins, O. L. Knight.
1893—O. C. Hopkins, O. L. Knight, A. S. Holman.
1894—D. W. Goding, A. S. Holman, G. L. Rowe.
1895—O. L. Knight, G. L. Rowe, A. S. Holman.
1896—A. S. Holman, H. Turner, D. W. Goding.

1897—J. W. Gowell, L. M. Wing, Chas. J. Tracy.

1898-'99—J. W. Gowell, H. R. Robinson, C. J. Tracy.

1900—J. W. Gowell, Job Merrill, N. G. McIntire.

1901—A. S. Holman, N. G. McIntire, R. S. Tracy.

1902—A. S. Holman, H. Turner, R. S. Tracy.

1903—A. S. Holman, H. Turner, H. O. Rowe.

1904—A. S. Holman, J. W. Gowell, Benj. Lovejoy.

1905—A. S. Holman, J. W. Gowell, A. B. McIntire.

## INDUSTRIES

The industrial life of Peru has been varied by the rise and fall of several lumber and grist mills, and by the steady development of her fertile though hilly farm lands. The enormous old-growth forest, which had stood for so long and served as the common home of the native Red Men, as soon as the whites entered the land to make homes for themselves fell a pray to the incessant chuck of their strong axes. The first openings were soon connected by narrow cuttings which served for highways, while here and there, along the noisy brooks were made larger openings where the trees, sometimes sawing boards three and four feet wide, had been cut down for timber and for the mills. The streams served a three-fold purpose; the falls provided the power to drive the saws, the body of water formed by the stream being dammed to make the power available was used for a

"log-yard" while the flowing waters brought saw logs to the mill.

The earliest mill at Peru Center was built by James Lunt about the time of the incorporation of the town. This was both a saw and grist mill. The sawing was done by an up-and-down saw. Mr. Lunt afterward sold the property to a Mr. Wagg, who operated it for a time and sold to a Mr. Johnson. About 1840, Robinson Turner, father of Hollis Turner, to whom we are indebted for much of this information, purchased the old mill, rebuilt it and put in Burr stones for a wheat mill. This was, it is said, the first wheat mill in the county. Mr. Turner operated the mills until about 1864, when he sold to a Mr. Silver. It then changed hands several times, was again built over, this time by Gustavus Hayford, of Canton, and has been owned and operated by Howard Turner about 10 years. It is now chiefly a custom sawing mill.

The early town records mention constructing a bridge at "Curtis' mill," but we are unable to give its location. There was an early saw mill at the outlet of Worthley Pond, which was built by Wm. K. Ripley. The mill is now obliterated.

The mill below the bridge at East Peru was an early corn or grist mill, built by Daniel Deshon. It was closed for many years, or was occupied as a wheelwright shop until sold to Thomas Farrar who changed it to a mill for sawing spool stock and dowels. Above the bridge is another mill containing a shingle machine and circular board saw. Job House turned bowls here around 1840. It has been in the

hands of several operators; E. M. Howard being the present owner.

At West Peru a saw mill was built about 1857, by Demas Bishop and John Jenne. Mr. Bishop operated the saw, clapboard and shingle mills, and in summer threshed his neighbors' grain at the mill. Mr. Jenne was a cabinet maker and occupied the second story of the mill. He also made window blinds and sashes. Mr. Jenne came to this town in 1822 from Hallowell, walking with three brothers, Joseph, Isaac and Seth, himself being but ten years old at that time. Mr. Jenne sold his interest in the mill to Mr. Bishop, and Mr. Bishop later sold to Tristram Washburn. A. C. Small was the next owner. He was also a grocer at the west village, and the donator of the Free Baptist church. The mill was sold by his executors to E. G. Austin, and was operated by E. G. Austin & Son, until just prior to its being burned last spring. J. A. Putnam, who bought a half interest in the property before the fire is now the sole owner, and is erecting a new mill on the old site. The new mill will be considerably smaller than its predecessor and will be occupied for manufacturing long and short lumber.

Joseph A. Arnold moved to West Peru from Rumford about twenty years ago and purchased the grist mill of Ira Parlin. Mr. Arnold operated the mill until his death last November, since which time it has been operated by his sons under the name of Arnold Bros.

Hall Bros.' rake manufacturing establishment, located about three-fourths of a mile from West Peru station on the river road has been established for several years, shipments

# MILITARY ACCOUNT

It is said that Major Wm. Brackett, who was one of the pioneers in this town, had served in the war for American Independence. We know of no others who settled in Peru, who fought in the Revolution. Mr. Brackett lived in this town for many years; he returned to Westbrook in 1845, at the advanced age of 93.

Three veterans of the War of 1812-14 lie buried in Peru: John Gilcrease, John Tufts, who fought at Plattsburg, and Thomas Lord, whose home was in that part of Peru formerly belonging to Franklin Plantation.

The town was well represented in the War of the Rebel-lion, and the records made by her noble sons are such as to do honor to this liberty-loving people. Demeritt Post, No. 147 is the local order of the few remaining veterans of this war, but most of them have answered the last roll-call on earth. The following is a list of the men credited to the town by the Adjutant General of Maine.

### LIST OF SOLDIERS, 1861-65

John Austin, Chas. A. Austin, Lieut. E. S. Bisbee, Jesse Bishop, Elisha S. Bisbee, Wm. H. Bent, Edwin Babb, Francis Burgess, Geo. D. Bisbee, Hannibal Bisbee, Jeremiah C. Brackett, Ephraim C. Benson, Wm. M. Bishop, Jas. A. Barrows, Stillman W. Bailey, Levi N. Bonney, Albert S. Benson, Homer Child, Wm. Canwell, Elihu Child, Wm. Cox, Ephraim Conant, Oliver B. Canway, Lester H. Chase, Oliver B. Canwell, Asa Childs, Geo. V. Childs, John A. Caldwell, Chas. G. Delano, Chas. C. Demerritt, P. O. Darrington, Chas. H. Derborne, Arthur L. Decoster, Chas. A. Deshon, Dan'l D. Delano, Chas. Frost, Jr., Wm. Frost, Sylvester Frost, Benj. F. Frost, Chas. J. Frost, Lysander P. Foster, Jas. M. Gammon, Jas. H. Gammon, Roscoe Gammon, Otis C. Holt, Jas. H. Hammon, Jos. B. Harmon, Geo. W. Haskell, Edw. W. Haines, Rollins Harmon, Geo. O. Hayford, Orland A. Hayford, Wm. Harlow, Jr, Josiah S. Hodgdon, Benj. R. Irish, Sam'l F. Irish, Jas. S. Jewett, Gardiner Lovejoy, Edwin A. Lane, Wm. F. Lombard, Peter H. Mitchell, Zavier Martin, Walter S. Newton, Roscoe G. Newell, John Oldham, Jas. B. Pollard, Louis O. Poland, Ellis Ripley, Seth Roberts, Corp. O. W.

Robinson, Henry Rowe, Roscoe Smith, Benj. Smith, Romanzo O. Stockbridge, Colby Sampson, Dan'l W. Sampson, Wheeler Tracy, Wm. H. Trask, Hanibal S. Tucker, Oscar M. Tucker, Hollis Turner, Lieut. Henry B. Walton, Ephraim Weitzler, Geo. H. Watson, Corp'l Farwell Walton, Thos. Wyman, Geo. W. Warren, Alfred B. Walker, Benj. F. Walton, Chas. F. York.

Nor was this town without representation in the late Spanish-American war. Orlando A. Bisbee, a member of one of Peru's respected families served in this war, but enlisted from the State of Massachusetts. Since the war closed he has returned to this town and is now a resident of Dickvale.

## RELIGIOUS ORGANIZATIONS.

What was the very earliest organized religious body in town we are unable to say. Certain it is that the settlers generally were a devoted and church-going people, did not neglect to assemble themselves together on the Lord's Day, nor to provide preaching of the doctrine most to their liking. The long forenoon sermon was followed by an equally long afternoon service, after which some of the sturdy settlers must return eight or ten miles with their families on ox-sleds. These services were held in private homes, or,

later, in the "village school house," until a suitable house
could be erected and dedicated solely to the worship of God.

The earliest meeting house erected in town was built by
the METHODISTS and dedicated in 1838. This is the same
building now used by the Baptists at Peru Center, it having
remained in posession of the Methodists until about eight
years ago when it was sold to the present occupants. The
exact date of organizing the Methodist Episcopal Society
we are unable to give, but believe it was previous to 1818,
when the Baptist society was formed. In the town records
for the first year after organization we find the town follows
the old custom of calling a minister, and voting him a sal-
ary and ministerial lands. The call was extended to Enoch
Jaques, who seems to have accepted the call, and became an
esteemed and valued pastor and citizen. This was a strong
society for many years but has now become nearly extinct,
caused by deaths and removals from town.

THE BAPTIST CHURCH was organized Sept. 19, 1818, at
the house of Bro. Benjamin Wormell, at East Peru, the following nine members forming the body: Jabez Delano and
Grace, his wife; Brady Bailey and Nancy, his wife; Benj Wormell and Annie, his wife; Robinson Turner, Gilbert Hatha-
way, and Sampson Freeman. At first services were held in
the Brady schoolhouse and other schoolhouses in town,
services being conducted by supply pastors or lay preachers. Later they began worshipping in the church they now
own, alternating with the Methodists and Free Baptists.
Gradually the Methodists became weakened and finally discontinued their services, and the Free Baptists erected a

at the west village, so, in 1894, the Baptists pur-
the sacred structure, repaired and extensively re-
l it, and soon began something like regular worship;
uckson, Palmer, Haines and others filling the pulpit.
earlier preachers we would mention Rev. Elias Nelson
ited with the church in 1830, and filled the pulpit
the time for three years. Rev. S. S. Wyman became
t settled pastor, in 1843. He settled in the town and
ed until his death, serving the society long and well.
. H. S. Ventres came from Canton in 1885 and re-
pastor two years. Preaching is now generally had
e pastors of the Canton Baptist church. Some Cobb
y students are employed. Rev. E. A. Davis, State
ary from Lewiston, now fills the pulpit occasionally.
ay School is maintained most of the time. The so-
w numbers but twenty. Were the earnest zeal of
ers continued by the present generations the old
would yet be the scene of great religious interest and
y; let us hope the time will speedily come when this may
zed and the entire community seek God's house on
ly Day.

Second Advent Church of Peru, located at Dickvale,
ganized in 1872 with the following members:

iel Abbott, Sally Abbott, Fidelia Abbott, A. A.
, Salmon Andrews, Aaron Andrews, Mary Andrews,
Bodwell, Mrs. E. Bodwell, daughter, F. Childs,
Eastman, Wheeler Tracy, Mary Tracy, Willis Gowell,
lle Tracy, Eliza Tracy, Lorenzo McAlister, Abbie
ter, Eliza McAlister, Mattie McAlister, Lewis Putnam,

Almon Andrews, M. J. Andrews, Eben Hopkins, Cynthia Hopkins, Edward Johnson, S. M. Locke, E. T. Locke, Carrie Locke.

From 1872 to 1905, Rev. A. A. Abbott has been the faithful pastor of this church. During his absence from 1894 to 1899, Rev. L. C. Putnam supplied. It was eleven years after the organization of the church that their building was erected, those in charge being Rev. A. A. Abbott, L. C. Putnam, Granville Child and John A. Putnam. The first meeting held in this structure was on July 4, 1893. The following fall the house was dedicated, the dedicatory sermon being preached by Kate Taylor. There are no regular services held in this church at the present time. The present membership is twenty. No account of this church would be complete without a brief reference to Rev. Mr. Abbott, its faithful pastor, now 78 years of age. During his long and active life he has preached 1300 funeral sermons, married more than 400 couples, and the number baptised by his hands is so large that he has long since forgotten the exact figures. Few men can point to a record more replete with activity and service than his.

## EDUCATION

Impelled by the thought of advancement, the pioneers of Maine were not blind to the demand for education. Hardly had they become located in the wilderness before some means was sought to offer their boys and girls the meagre

instruction which was within their power to offer. It is probable that private schools, or schools supported by subscription, with the instructor "boarding round", were sustained prior to the organization of the Plantation in 1812. Certain it is that very soon after its organization the voters in the plantation provided systematic instruction, for in 1813 $50 was raised for the support of schools, and the "Lower", "Upper", and "Western" districts laid out by a specially appointed committee. The following year a similar amount was appropriated for this purpose, but in 1815 nothing was raised for schools. Schools were had, however, and it is to be presumed that suitable "masters" could not be found to teach the full time the preceding years. Three "school wards" were chosen each year to attend to the expenditure of the school funds. In 1816 a school house was erected at the "Senter" and the three districts were consolidated, those who could not attend the school here were to receive "some consideration". Robinson Turner, James Lunt, Adam Knight, Hezekiah Walker and Wm. Brackett were chosen a committee to superintend building the house. We find it completed the next year, when it was occupied for holding a plantation meeting; this stood on what became known as Town House Hill, the house having been used for a town house for many years after the incorporation of Peru.

But the plan of a single school district was not satisfactory to many who lived at a distance with no means of travel but to walk. Several attempts were made to re-district the township, which was done in 1819, when four dis-

tricts were established, named the Upper, Lower, Center, and Back districts.

From this beginning an efficient and practical school system has developed, new districts were laid out from time to time as the demands of the pupils required. After the passage of the law for town ownership and management of schools, many of the districts having but few scholars, some of them were consolidated, but this time transportation was provided for those at a distance from the school.

Union Hall was erected at West Peru, in 1860, and is a substantial two-story brick structure containing a public hall, and a school room. A new school building and town hall was erected in 1896-7 at Peru village, and another school building has just been completed in what is now called the Union School District. This will be occupied in the fall by the High school to be re-established at that time. Sessions of High school have been held in town; in 1880 we find there were High schools at both the West village and at the Center, but these have been discontinued for a few years.

A graded system has been recently established at the Center school, the Grammar school graduating its first class this season. The class was a large one, and held its exercises on Independence Day. The public schools of this town have helped many boys and girls who have later reached positions of prominence and trust, whom Peru is proud to call her sons and daughters, to lay the foundation for an education which has enabled them to become leaders among men.

## PATRONS OF HUSBANDRY.

Rockemeka Grange, Number 109, was organized at Peru, in the Baptist church, Feb. 19, 1875, with 30 charter members. The order was soon removed to West Peru, but later returned to Peru, and has since removed to the West Village, then back again April 23, 1898, since which time its meetings have been held at the Center Village. The meetings were for a time held in the Town Hall, until the new Grange Hall was dedicated on June 10, 1904. This hall was erected at a cost of over $2,000. It is well furnished. There are now 103 members. Meetings are held weekly, on Saturday evening. The present principal officers are O. C. Hopkins, Master; Thos. J. Rolls, Overseer; Mrs. A. B. Walker, Lecturer; Mrs. C. T. Gammon, Secretary; G. W. Knight, Treasurer; and Mrs. Thos. Farrar, Chaplain.

The following is a complete list of past Masters of this Grange, with their dates of service: Wm. Greene, 1875; Merrill Knight, '76; Wm. H. Walker, '77; A. B. Walker, '78-'80; Wm. H. Walker, '81-'82; A. B. Walker, '83-'85; Frank P. Putnam, '86-'87; A. B. Walker '88; D. W. Walker, '89; Hollis Turner, '90; Roscoe S. Tracy, '91; C. A. Hall, '92-'93; Manderville Hall, '94-'96; A. B. Walker, '97-'98; Loren E. Irish, '99-'00; Dana W. Goding, '01; J. E. Conant, '02-'03; A. B. Walker, '04; O. C. Hopkins, '05·

West Peru Grange, Number 391, was organized with 69 charter members, on May 10, 1902. Its membership

has increased to 156, in three years, and the work done by the order shows much enterprise. It now owns the brick hall at the West Village, where its meetings are held on the first and third Saturdays of each month. Manderville Hall was chosen first Master; Chas. A. Hall, Secretary; C. M. Small, Overseer; and Mrs. F. L. Phinney, Lecturer. Chas. A. Hall became the second Master, and was in turn succeeded by John E. Goggin, now in office. Manderville Hall is the present Lecturer and Marcia V. Hall is Secretary.

The Petition of Samuel Butterfield of Dunstable, for himself, and in behalf of several persons here after named. For a tract of land now the property of this State, lying and being in the County of Cumberland and joining (has) Northerly Lands Petitioned for by Abijah Buck and others, and Northeasterly of No. Four (Paris). To the value of six miles square or a sufficient number of Acres for a town to be laid out as agreeable to your Petitioners as maybe— upon such consideration or for such a sum as you in your Wisdom shall think best for the good of this State, your Petitioners Being Desirous of Making a Settlement on Said Land if granted, which not only would be a Benefit to them- Selves but to the Community at Large and the Wilderness become a fruitful field your Petitioners relying on your Wisdom, care and Tenderness Pray the Above Said Lands may be granted as you in your Great Wisdom may Direct.

Your Petitioners as in Duty Bound Shall Ever Pray. Janu_
ary the 24th 1781. (Signed)

> SAMUEL BUTTERFIELD,
> ALEXANDER PAYSON,
> MARK HOBBS and others.

The above petition seems to have been for Township
No. 6 which formed the southern half of the double town_
ship of Butterfield, now the towns of Hartford and Sum_
ner. We are unable to say what later petition was made
but both Numbers 6 and 7 were granted these petitioners
not long after.

The earliest meeting of the Proprietors was held May 1,
1788, at the house of Ebenezer Bancroft in Dunstable. Mr.
Bancroft was chosen proprietary clerk. Three agents were
then chosen to act in behalf of the proprietors, selection of
Mr. Bancroft, Samuel Butterfield and Peter Coburn being
made, they being instructed to settle with those settlers
who were entitled to a hundred acres of land in Buttefield or
No. 6 and No. 7, as formerly granted by the General Court.
Sept. 22, 1791 the proprietors voted to accept the plan and
report of this committee and to enter the same on the pro-
prietors' records. Allotments were by them made, and recorded, to the following men who had already settled in the
township: "In the West town to James Keen, Hezekiah
Stutson, John Briggs, Isaac Sturtivant, Benj. Haild, John
Crokit, Moses Buck, Oliver Cummings, Jun'r, John Bisbee,
John Fletcher, Levi Crocket, Simeon Basset, John Keen,
Moses Bisbee, Joshua Ford, and Simeon Parlin."

"In the East town to Asa Robinson, Wm. Heaford, In-

crease Roberson, Mesbek Keen, Joseph Roberson, Wm. Tucker, Isaac Bonney, John Bonney, Charles Bisbee, David Oldham, Charles Ford, Elisha Bisbee, Noah Bozworth."

It will be seen from the above that Butterfield Town. ship, which was composed of township No. 6 in the south and township No. 7 in the north, was early divided into two sections by a line r u n n i n g north and south or at nearly right angles to the old line. This was nearly parallel to the general course of the river which was originally the dividing line between Hartford and Sumner. These were then dis. tinctively called the East Town and the West Town, later East and West Butterfield plantations.

Several p e t i t i o n s were made to the General Court of Massachusetts by the East and West townships. The first petition was made by West Butterfield May 1, 1793, which was followed by one from the Settlers in the Eastern plan. tation dated Aug. 22, the same year, and was signed by In. crease Robinson, Wm. Hayford, Isaac Bonney, Wm. Soule and Charles Foord. Both seem to have been rejected, as were also a second from the West plantation issued the following December; a second from East Butterfield dated December 21st, 1795 and signed by forty taxpayers (the name d e s i r e d w a s "Lisbon if it may be and if not Hartford"); a third petition from West Butterfield in Jan. 1796 which was signed by 29 taxpayers; a fourth petition, dated December 18, 1797, and asking that the river be the dividing line; a petition for the incorporation of both plantations as one town, dated Dec. 19, 1797; and a third petition by East Butterfield, April 7th, 1798, with the river as the

dividing line. The range line first adopted as the division between the townships gave the Eastern township 8365 acres more than its Sister town. With the river the dividing line the difference in area was reduced to 4475 acres. Very soon after the last mentioned petition was made a joint petition was sent by the two plantations for their separate incorporation. This met the approved of the General Court and both towns, the Eastern taking the name of Hartford, and the western the name of Sumner, were duly incorporated.

## SETTLEMENT.

The first settlements were made within the bounds of old Butterfield plantation under an act passed by the Massachusetts legislature giving 100 acres of land to any who would clear sixteen acres back from the rivers or navigable waters within four years. This offer continued until 1784, prior to which date there seem to have been no less than thirteen claims taken up in the East township by the men whose names are given in the last chapter. These men located wherever they chose since no general survey was made in this vicinity until 1785 when John Jordine surveyed for the State the present town of Buckfield, and the southern half of the present Hartford and Sumner, then called "No 6".

The following year "No 7" was surveyed by Samuel Titcomb for the State. On June 22, of that year (1786), a Deed of Agreement was made between the State's committee and Joel Parkhurst of Dunstable, Mass., and his associates, and on Nov. 22, 1787 this deed, which conveyed townships No. 6 and No. 7 upon payment of the price specified, was given to Ebenezer Bancroft of Dunstable, and his associates, 43 in number; to whom most of the land titles in these towns may be traced.

According to the "Sumner Centennial" history twenty one settlers had taken up claims and made permanent improvements within the limits of the old plantation. Of this number, Benj. Heald, Oliver Cummings and Increase Robinson became proprietors.

Our limited space does not permit us to make extended comment concerning the pioneers of this town. We give the following as the most important facts concerning these noble men. Of the thirteen mentioned in the preceding chapter who received deeds of 100 acres each as settlement rights, Deacon Increase Robinson erected and operated mills at what is now East Sumner, the mills remaining in the town of Hartford until the dividing line between the towns was changed. A separate section of land around Whitney pond was surveyed by Noah Bosworth, one of these men, for two Thompson Cousins, and two other men, all of Middleboro, Mass. This was known as Thompson's Grant and became part of North Hartford except a small portion now in Canton. The first settlers in this part of the town were four Thompsons, two sons of each of the gran-

tees. These men were known as Dea. Oakes, Dea. Ira, Esq.
John, and Esq. Cyrus Thompson. The first settled on the
farm formerly occupied by Mrs. Alvira Mendall. Oakes Jr.
remained on the place after his father. Dea. Ira settled on
the hill just west of Whitney Pond, on the "Ellis farm," he
afterwards exchanged farms with Perez Ellis of Livermore.
Esq. John settled on the John Manwell place. He afterwards exchanged farms with Uzza Thompson of Rumford.
Esq. Cyrus settled the farm afterwards used as a townfarm,
where the buildings were burned in 1883. He married
Rebecca Robinson, the first female white child born in Sumner. They had four children. Uzza Thompson who removed
from Rumford as we have stated, married Abigail Elliott,
who had seven children. Perez Ellis, who came from No.
Livermore had seven sons and six daughters.

Lemuel Thomas settled north of the Ellis farm, near the
Canton line. Ebenezer Washburn located on the farm next
west of Wm. Thomas, beginning life here in a log cabin.
Joseph Soule, of Middleboro, located next south west of Mr.
Washburn, where he was succeeded by Ezra, his son, who
became a lieutenant in the Civil War. Wm. Thomas settled
an adjoining lot. Capt. Nathaniel Thomas made his home
on the farm now occupied by Mr. York. Elisha Thomas
purchased an adjoining lot and became a black- and gun-
smith. He married Betsey, daughter of Ebenezer Washburn, by whom he had twelve children. Zeri Haylord settled
in this locality, but soon sold to Thomas Allen and moved
to Canton (then Jay). Other early arrivals in North Hartford were Wm. Sparrow, Andrew Barrows, Moses Fletcher,

Josiah Tilson, Simeon Brown, Daniel Thomas, Moses Sampson, Beza Soule, Lemuel Jewett, Osborn Trask and Woodward Allen.

In the southern part of the town Wm. Baird planted a field of corn in 1788 from which he harvested a crop which he took back in his pockets, the bears, deer and other animals having preceded him. Soon after this he became a permanent settler. Edmund Irish then spelled Yrish who has had the reputation of being the earliest permanent settler built a log cabin on the farm now occupied by Decatur Irish, his grandson, to which he moved his family in 1788. Richard Dearborn, David Warren, and James Ricker, each settled early in southern Hartford, on farms now occupied by their respective grandsons. Daniel Hutchinson was an early Baptist Preacher. He and Mr. Warren were each sent to represent this town in the Massachusetts Legislature. Barnabus Howard, Zenas Mitchell, Richard Young, Stephen Irish, Christian Christianson and Daniel Briggs were all early arrivals in this section.

Edward Blake located in the south east part of the town, the Larrabees in the eastern part. John Bartlett purchased 90 acres here in 1793 and moved in with his wife and seven children. Benj. Thomas settled where T. B. W. Stetson now lives. Andrew and Jeremiah Russell were here early. Ephraim Tinkham, Nathaniel Fogg, and the Bryants, Guerneys and Starbirds made their clearings in the central part of the town.

Other early names in the history of this town, men who played a leading part in its early development are Malachi

Bartlett, Freeman Ellis, Wm. Soule, Arvida Hayford, John
Pumpilly, John Elwell, Joseph Chandler, John Ames, David
Parsons, Samuel Ellery, Andrew Cushman, Nathaniel Bart-
lett, Jonathan Bozworth, Borgillai Hollis, Richard Hinds,
John Briggs, Benj. Heath, John Griffith, Sampson Reed,
Meader Blake, and Anson Soule.

Dr. Smith was probably the earliest practicing physician.
Others have been Dr. Washington Bragg, and Dr. Lemuel
H. Maxim, who died two or three years ago, There is now
no resident physician in town.

Legal business transactions have generally been done
by local Justices of the peace. We believe the town has had
no practicing representative of the school of law.

## INCORPORATION

COPY OF FIRST TOWN WARRANT

### COMMONWEALTH OF MASSACHUSETTS

To William Hayford of Hartford, in said County yoman
    greeting.

In persuance of a Law of this Commonwealth directing
me to issue my warrant to some suitable inhabitant of said
Hartford I do hereby Request you forthwith to notify and
warn the inhabitants of said Hartford to Meet at your
Dwelling house on Monday The thirteenth day of August

next at ten of the clock in the forenoon then & their to Chose all such officers as towns are by Law Required to choose in the Month of March or April annually and Make Return of this warrant and your doings Theirof to the Moderator and Town Clerk That shall then and their be Chosen. given under my hand and seale Dated At Sumner the twenty-third day of July in the year of our Lord one thousand Seven hundred and ninety Eight.

ISAAC STURTEVANT *J'ts Ps*

The first town meeting of the inhabitants of Hartford was held accordingly, at Wm. Hayford's residence on August 13, 1798. Mr. Hayford was chosen to act as Moderator; Malachi Bartlett, clerk; which office he continued to fill until 1802, when Arvida Hayford was chosen his successor. Freeman Ellis, William Soule and Andrew Russell were chosen selectmen, and then made assessors. Malachi Bartlett was also chosen town treasurer. Arvida Hayford became collector, and was elected a constable, John Pumpilly and John Elwell were selected to act as fence viewers, and Joseph Chandler, John Elwell, John Ames, and Wm. Soule, as road surveyors. David Parsons and Beza Soule were chosen (tideingmen) tythingmen. Samuel Ellery and John Bartlett became hogreves, and Andrew (Chusman) Cushman a surveyor of lumber. The meeting was then "Desolved."

On January 5th, 1799, a warrant was issued by the selectmen directing Arvida Hayford, constable, to give notice to John Parlen, with his wife and children, having taken up their residence in the town without the town's consent, to "depart the limits thereof within fifteen days."

On July 26, 1819, a final vote of the town was taken on the question of establishing an independent State. Of the 66 votes cast, just two-thirds were in favor of the measure. Joseph Tobin was sent a delegate to represent the town in the Convention at Portland.

ACT OF INCORPORATION

## COMMONWEALTH OF MASSACHUSETTS

In the year of our Lord, one thousand, seven hundred & ninety eight.

An Act to incorporate the Plantation called East Butterfield in the County of Cumberland into a Town by the name of Hartford.

Sect. 1. Be it Enacted by the Senate and House of Representatives in General Court assembled & by the Authority of the same, That the Plantation of East Butterfield in the County of Cumberland, Bounded as follows, vizt. . . . . beginning at the Northeast Corner of Buckfield, thence running North, twenty six degrees East two miles and three hundred rods, to the Northeast Corner of Turner; thence North, three miles & two hundred and sixty rods; thence North, eighty one degrees West, four miles & one hundred & sixty rods; thence North sixty five degrees West, one mile and two hundred & twenty eight Rods to the middle of the East branch of Twenty Mile River so called; thence down the middle of said River to the North line of Buckfield; thence South, eighty one degreess East, three miles and two hundred & sixty six Rods adjoining Buckfield, to the first

Bound, with the Inhabitants thereon, be and they hereby are Incorporated into a Town by the name of Hartford. And the said Town is hereby vested with all the Powers, Privileges & immunities, which other Towns in this Commonwealth do or may by law enjoy.

Sect. 2. Be it further Enacted, that Isaac Sturdivant Esq. be and he hereby is empowered to issue his Warrant directed to some suitable Inhabitant within said Town, requiring him to warn a Meeting of the Inhabitants thereof, at which time and place as shall be expressed in said Warrant, for the purpose of choosing such Town Officers as other Towns are empowered to choose in the Month of March or April annually.

June 13th 1798,

By the Governor,

Approved

INCREASE SUMNER.

---

## TOWN OFFICIALS

### SELECTMEN.

1850—Daniel Parsons, Stephen Thurlow, Jr., Hiram Hines.

1851—H. Hines, Cyrus Thompson, Jr., Wm. Irish.

1852—S. Thurlow, Jr., Deering Farrar, John Walker.

1853—John Walker, Wm. Irish, Nathaniel Thomas.

MPH5

1854—Wm. Irish, Hiram Hines, Wm. B. Sparrow.

1855—H. Hines, Wm. B. Sparrow, Benj. F. Cary.

1856—S. Thurlow, Jr., Benj. F. Cary, Zenas Holmes.

1857—S. Thurlow, Jr., Cyrus Ricker, Asa Robinson.

1858—S. Thurlow, Jr., Daniel Parsons, Lemuel Cole.

1859-'60—Daniel Parsons, Richard Hutchinson, Sampson Read.

1861—R. Hutchinson, James Glover, Oakes Thompson.

1862—S. Thurlow, Benj. F. Cary, John T. Glover.

1863—J. T. Glover, Benj. F. Cary, Merritt Parsons.

1864—Cyrus Ricker, S. Thurlow, Joseph S. Mendall.

1865—S. Thurlow, J. S. Mendall, Benj. F. Robinson.

1866—J. S. Mendall, Benj. F. Robinson, Stephen E. Irish.

1867—Merritt Parsons, J. F. Glover, Wm. R. Cary.

1868-'69—S. E. Irish, J. S. Mendall, Alden Barrell.

1870-'71—John T. Glover, Merritt Parsons, Moses Alley.

1872-'73—J. S. Mendall, Benj. F. Cary, I. E. Richardson.

1874-'76—J. S. Mendall, Benj. F. Cary, John T. Glover.

1877-'78—S. E. Irish, S. M. Stetson, H. C. Ricker.

1879—J. S. Mendall, C. Thomas, M. Russell.

1880-'82—S. E. Irish, J. M. Russell, J. W. Libby.

1883—S. E. Irish, J. M. Russell, T. B. W. Stetson.

1884—J. M. Russell, T. B. W. Stetson, J. T. Glover.

1885-'86—J. W. Libby, Frank L. Warren, C. Fletcher.

1887—T. B. W. Stetson, S. E. Irish, F. L. Warren.

1888—F. L. Warren, T. B. W. Stetson, Mellen Holmes.

1889—T. B. W. Stetson, Mellen Holmes, Emery Parsons.

1890—T. B. W. Stetson, Mellen Holmes, M. Alley.

1891—J. M. Russell, Amos Perkins, H. F. Irish.

1892—J. M. Russell, H. F. Irish, Mellen Holmes.

1893—J. M. Russell, H. F. Irish, J. T. Glover.

1894—J. M. Russell, F. L. Warren, C. C. Fletcher.

1895-'97—F. L. Warren, J. W. Libby, D. A. Fletcher.

1898—F. L. Warren, Benj. F. Cary, Chas. H. Berry.

1899-1900—T. B. W. Stetson, O. Turner, E. A. Skilling.

1901—John T. Glover, C. H. Berry, Frank Glover.

1902-'03—Frank Glover, C. H. Berry, J. M. Millett.

1904—C. H. Berry, Geo. A. Holmes, Thos. E. Ryerson.

1905—Z. W. Libby, W. H. Allen, G. E. Corliss.

### CLERKS

1875-1901, M. C. Osgood; 1902-5, T. B. W. Stetson.

### TREASURERS

1875-8, L. N. Thompson; 1879-87, M. C. Osgood; 1888-90, John Oldham; 1891, C. C. Fletcher; 1892-1901, M. C. Osgood; 1902-5, T. B. W. Stetson.

## CIVIL WAR SOLDIERS.

The town of Hartford has been well represented in the great national conflicts at arms. Many of the men who settled on her soil prior to 1800 were veterans of the Revolutionary War in which they displayed the spirit of Puritan valor and love of liberty, which lead their ancestors to establish their homes on the New England shore. Nor have succeeding generations been without the zeal of their an-

cestors. In the War of 1812, and in the great Civil Strife, were enlisted many of the men of Hartford who, by their noble records, she is proud to claim as her sons.

The following is a list of enlisted soldiers in the Civil War, as recorded by the Adjutant General of Maine, from 1861 to 1865:

### SOLDIERS OF HARTFORD.

Albert Allen, Albert L. Adderton, Chas. F. Allen, Edwin Andrews, Otis Bosworth, Lieut. Calvin B. Benson, Isaac R. Bubier, John M. Benson, Lucius C. Bartlett, Valorus A. Bearce, Rufus Bryant, Leander Bartlett, Leonard Bosworth, Jr., Jas. M. Cobb, Benj. M. Corliss, Levi C. Coburn; Lysander DeCoster, Benj. M. Callis, Albert A. Ellis, Christopher C. Fletcher, Elbridge H. Foster, Jas. E. Fogg, Hanson S. Field, Chas. A. Green, Stillman Guerney, Michael Guerney, Stephen C. Huntley, Andrew J. Hodgdon, Wm. M. Hall, Burnham Holmes, Wm. R. Hasey, Orman E. Hines, W. H. Irish, Florian Jordan, W. F. Jordan, Chas. Kearney, Adelbert Kidder, Chas. W. Mendall, Francis Leavitt, Caleb Mendall, Zepheniah H. Neal, Dennis Ricker, Jr., Justin H. Richardson, Wm. H. H. Richardson, Jas. M. Ricker, Dennis Ricker, Lucius Robinson, Ellis S. Russell, Jeremiah Russell, Ezra Soule, Jas. E. Starbird, Ephraim T. Stetson, E. P. Stetson, Sedate M. Turner, W. J. Tyler, John W. Thompson, Geo. B. Thompson, Jonathan Williams, John G. Wood, Geo. H. Wood, Lucius Young, Jos. H. Young, Delance Young, Henry Young and Edward L. Stephens.

# LOCAL INDUSTRIES

The earliest mill within the bounds of Hartford was erected at the Center village just above the railroad bridge where a part of the old dam may now be seen. A second mill was built by Winslow Hall below the present railroad station. This was a saw and grist-mill, and the village which sprung up became known as "Hall's Mills" until about 1838, when it was changed to Hartford Center. Wm. Hall was also postmaster when mails came but once a week. Hinds & Woodsum bought the mill of Mr. Hall and Harvey Bartlett. Later the mill run down and Robinson & Corliss purchased the site, erected a new mill with a mill for manufacturing excelsior which was shipped to Mechanic Falls, in 1865, for the first manufacture of paper. James Irish bought out Mr. Corliss and operated the mills with Mr. Robinson until the railroad was extended to Hartford from Buckfield in 1868 and this mill privilege bought for the site to bridge Bungamuck stream. The railroad reached Canton Jan. 1, 1870, but was not in shape to do business. Under F. O. J. Smith's management Hartford enjoyed few railroad conveniences. Mr. Smith died in 1876, after which Ex. Gov. Washburn, Otis Hayford, of Canton; N. L. Marshall, of West Paris; S. C. Andrews, of Buckfield; and James Irish, of Hartford took hold of the project and completed it in 1878. Many interesting stories are told of this road under its early management. The road-bed was poorly graded and the run from the lower end of the line to Can-

ton was such a task that the train gained for itself the name "the try-weekly"; the theory being that after the run down river it was a week's "try" to return.

Another dam was built about one mile below those mentioned upon which James Irish remembers a clover mill. It is probable that there were other motor mills in town during the early days.

The only saw mills now in town are steam mills. One of these is operated by E. C. Irish, on the north side of Bunga-muck Pond, but this is a portable mill. The other steam mill is operated by Mr. Littlefield.

The corn canning establishment of the Minot Packing Co., in the southeastern part of the town, was built by Gerry & Thurston about 1892, since which time it has been operated each season. A large business is done canning sweet corn which is raised by the farmers of the surround-ing section.

The business done by the Hartford Cold Spring Co., now the Hartford Mineral Spring Co., has been one of consider-able importance during the last twelve or fifteen years. This spring is located on the Daniel Briggs farm. Shipments were first made of the clear spring water, the analysis of which shows very superior quality. This is now used in making gingerale, soda water, etc., which is shipped in large quantities.

But the chief industries in town at the present time are farming and orcharding. The surface is generally broken but the hills are arable and fertile, and the soil strong and productive. Among the proprietors of the plantation was

one whose name has become a household word throughout New England; Col. Laommi Baldwin, the originator of the famous apple which bears his name. There are many large and excellent apple orchards in Hartford and the returns realized from the sale of their product during the productive seasons is gratifying indeed to the orchardists and farmers of the town.

## CHURCH AFFAIRS

A Baptist Church was organized very early in the history of this town by Elder Daniel Hutchinson, who lived in the southern part of the town. This church was an active Christian force for many years, sharing with the Methodists and Universalists the love and labors of a devoted people; but now the Methodist society is the only one holding regular services. Rev. E. S. Cudworth was, Rev. G. J. Palmer is pastor.

NOTE—We have endeavored for some time to obtain data on the churches, but have failed. If it finally is sent to us in time, it will be inserted at the back of the book.

Atheneum Hall, which was erected at the Center, with the town hall in 1871 by the Good Templars' Lodge, has been used for religious worship by various denominations, and sometimes a Sunday School is maintained here.

## HARTFORD SCHOOLS

One of the earliest matters attended to by the newly organized towns, was to make provision for establishing and maintaining a suitable school system for the promotion of education. A special committee was appointed to district the township, and their report is recorded in the town books, as follows: "District the first" to begin at Anson Soule's, thence over Swan Pond hill to Edmund Irish and Richard Young. District No. 2, beginning at John Bartlett's, thence running on the town road to Freeman Ellis' and to include Holmes (?), John Griffeth and the Russells. District No. 3, beginning at Andrew Cushman's and extending to Richard Hinds and to Wm. Hayford, Jr. District No. 4, included Richard Dearborn, Beza Soule and the inhabitants on Ames' Hill.

The sum of $60 was raised for the support of schools. This was placed in the hands of the committee whose duty it was to lay out the districts as recorded above, the committee consisting of John Pumpilly, John Elwell, and Gustavus Hayford. School agents were chosen for the several districts as follows; John Elwell, District No. 1; John Griffith, District No. 2; Wm. Hayford, District No. 3; and Sampson Reed, Dist. No. 4.

Of the instructors employed in the early schools in Hartford and during succeeding years Wm. Bicknell was perhaps the best known in the town. His home was on the Daniel Briggs farm, where the mineral spring is located. He was a

successful "school master," author, and school superintend-
ent; and was a man much looked up to in those days. He
was born in 1804, in the town of Turner, but spent most of
his life here. John Larrabee was another early master,
under whose tuition James Irish sat. He was an excellent
penman and systematic in his methods. He was employed
as town clerk for many years. Another school teacher who
has a record seldom excelled, is Laura F., the daughter of
John Jenne, of Peru, now Mrs. James Irish. Between 1869
and 1900, she taught eighty-two schools, covering every
district from East Sumner to Rumford Falls.

When the district system was in force, there were four-
teen complete and two joint districts in this town; this
number has now decreased to eight districts, viz.: Line,
Center, Tyler's Cor., Union, Town Farm, Whiting, Moun-
tain and Glover. None of these schools are graded. A local
High school has been maintained in town, but High school
students are now generally sent to Hebron Academy or to
Leavitt Institute, their tuition being paid by the town.

We would mention here, in connection with education,
and to close this brief account, the fine library and chapel of
Rev. Lucjen Robinson, at his summer residence on the old
homestead of his grandfather, about a mile and a half from
the Center. Here he has an up-to-date library of 6000 vol-
umes, of which he leaves a choice selection at the postoffice
for those of the townspeople upon the payment of two cents
per book to the postmaster who is librarian. It is said the
library and building are to be devoted to Hartford and
Sumner, together with a fund for its maintainance, by Mr.

Robinson, who is a tutor in Philadelphia and a clergyman. The name he has selected for the valuable educational insti-tution which his townsmen must highly appreciate, is the East and West Butterfield Public Library, chosen in mem-ory of the sister plantations in whose development his fam-ily has played so prominent a part.

---

# DELAYED DATA

### FIRST BAPTIST CHURCH, MEXICO.

The Baptist church was organized at Mexico with thir-teen members, on May 29, 1903, Rev. J. D. Graham was in-stalled pastor at that time and remained with the church until Sept. 19. He was succeeded by the present pastor, Rev. Albert G. Warner, in October. The membership of this society has increased to twenty at the present time. Ser-vices are held at the church at Mexico Corner, and a success-ful Sunday School maintained.

We regret that we are unable to give accounts of the METHODIST CHURCH OF HARTFORD and the FREE BAPTIST CHURCH at WEST PERU. We have tried to obtain the necessary information but have been unable to do so.

# Census-1905

The population of the Towns of Mexico, Peru and Hartford has been arranged in families where that arrangement has been possible. In these families, in addition to the resident living members, the names of the non-resident members are included. It should be borne in mind that this plan does not include the names of all former residents of this town, as the names of the non-residents appear only when one or both of the parents are still living in the town. After the name of each non-resident will be found the present address, when such address has been given to us. Non-residents are indicated by the (*).

When a daughter in a family has married, her name taken in marriage appears after her given name in parenthesis, the name preceded by a small m, thus: (m     ).

Following the names of the population is the occupations. To designate these we have used the more common abbreviations and contractions, as follows: Farmer—far; carpenter—car; railroad service—R R ser; student, a member of an advanced institution of learning—stu; pupil, a member of a lower grade of schools (including all who have reached the age of five years)—pl; housework—ho; laborer—lab; physician and surgeon—phy & sur; clergyman—clerg; merchant—mer; teacher—tr; blacksmith—blk; clerk—cl; bookkeeper—bk kpr; lawyer—law; mechanic—mech; machinist—mach; engineer—eng; maker—mkr; worker—wkr; work—wk; shoe shop work—shoe op; cotton or woolen mill operatives —mill op; weaver—weav; spinner—spin; electrician—elec; painter—ptr; carriage work—car wk; dress maker—dr mkr; insurance—ins; traveling salesman, or commercial traveler—sales, or coml trav; music teacher—mus tr; teamster—team; general work—genl wk; mariner—mar; employ—emp; retired retd; fisherman—fisher; quarryman—quarry; contractor and builder—cont and bld; lumberman—lumb; factory work—fact wk; retired sea captain—rtd sea capt, or ex-sea capt; foreman—fore; fireman—fire.

This Census was taken expressly for this work during the Summer of 1905, by B. V. Davis, of Kent's Hill, Me.

# CENSUS OF MEXICO

TE.—Where address is not given **MEXICO** Post Office
·stood. The following abbreviations designate other
es of people living in Mexico: Dixfield—Dix; Rumford
R Falls; Ridlonville—Rid. Frye and Hale are also
fices in the town of Mexico.

| A | | | |
|---|---|---|---|
| , Elizabeth A (Foster | | Anna I | pl |
| a A (m Binford | ho | Thelma J | pl |
| Nathan D bk kpr | Rid | Andrews, Cedora J (Chadburn |
| rriet (Learned | ho | | Rid |
| rjorie | | Inez M | stu |
| Levi | cl | Walter H | pl |
| ell M (Lapsie | ho | Frank P | pl |
| lie J | | Armiatage, William | mill op |
| rge H | | Agnes M (Romans | ho |
| eo C blk | Rid | Fannie E | |
| ry L (Porter | ho | David W | |
| orge O | blk | Austin, J R far & milk dlr |
| rry B | eng | | Rid |
| hur H | pl | Alton A | stu |
| est P | pl | Carroll D | far |
| nie L · | mill op | Emily H (Keene · | ho |
| rvey R | pl | Austin, Hermon D | mill op |
| th A | | | Rid |
| dys M | | Idella M (Green | ho |
| Della (Knapp | Rid | B | |
| rbert L truckman | | | |
| on, Andrew pulp mill | | Babb, Fred L stone mason |
| | Rid | Clara M (Mosher | ho |
| ta (Martenson | ho | Muriel S | |

Marion L ) twins
Jessie E )
Babb, Emily J (Marsh ho
 *Flora L (m Merrill Bethel
 Etta G (m Howard ho
 Fred L stone mason
 Helen N (m Rodgerson ho
 Arthur W lab
Babb, D W retd Rid
 Olevia (Gale ho
 Silvia M (m Tripp ho
Babb, A W truckman Rid
 George W
Bagle, Jas E lumb
 Bessie B (Brennick ho
 Margaret M pl
 George A pl
 Grace V pl
Bailey, Lorenzo mill op Rid
 Drana S (Small ho
 *Lizzie M (m Howard ho
  Bridgton
 Lilla A mill op
Baker, H J plumb & steam fit
 Effie (Young ho
 Roy H
 Leon D
Balch, Frank F car Rid
 H A (Pushee
 West S
Barrett, Edwin retd Hale
 *A J eng Lynn, Mass
 *W R ss op Lynn, Mass
 Louisa ho

 *P G mer Peru Ctr
 Edwin Jr far
Barry, Robt A far Rid
 Ethel L (Knapp ho
 Percy J pl
 John L pl
 Robert C
Bates, Henry mill op Rid
Bean, N B master mach Rid
 Emma L (Libby ho
 Jennie E stu
 Carrie L pl
 Lena A pl
Bean, H E boss mach shop
  Rid
 Elzira B (Bennett ho
 Frank L mach
Bean, Julia A (Scribner Rid
 *John E eng Norway
 *Ann K (m Whitney ho
  Norfolk, Mass
 *Eunice E (m Gallagher
  Grand Junction, Col
 Henry B mach
 *Wm cab mkr Rid
 *Malerne (m Morgan
  Cambridge, Mass
 *Caroline M (m Goodnow
  West Bethel
 *Chas miner Leadville, Col
 *Augusta (m House ho
  East Wales
 N B master mach

*Frank L    R R ser
    Danville Junct
Beaudette, Duffy    team
    Flora (Lemey    ho
    Mary Ann
    Edna
Beedy, L A    far & car    Rid
    Eva B (Haines    ho
    *Bessie A (m Holt
        E Wilton
    Carson L    ptr
    Freeland F    ptr
    Flossie E    ho
    Ritter M    pl
    Wilfred F    pl
Bellar, Mary (Johnson    Rid
Bellows, W C    mach    R Falls
    Ella A (Rich    ho
    Warren R
Benard, Archie    mill op
    Jane (Galge    ho
Benard, Albert    car
    Sarah (Assanabut    ho
    Minnie    pl
    Lora
    Genie
    Josie
Bennett, Susan M (Chadwick
    Clara A (m Foley    ho
Bennett, M E    mill op
    Grace L    pl
Berry, Fred C    surveyor    Rid
    Mabel A (Caswell    ho
    Edith M    pl

Ruby F    pl
Rena E    pl
Besaw, John    far & mason
    Annie (Fonier    ho
    Edie    ho
    William    cook
    Charles    mill op
    Lora (m Englord    ho
    Annie    mill op
    Rodol    pl
    Vina    pl
    Edmond    pl
Binford, H J    phy & sur
    Victor A    stu
    Lula A (Abbott    ho
Bishop, Lillian I (Walker    Rid
    Harry J    pl
    Lester A    pl
Blacquer, Peter
    Ellen (m Carey    ho
Blake, Thos J    mill op    Rid
Blake, Ida E (Chambers    ho
    *Ida M (m York    Roxbury
    James Scott
    William    lab
    Thomas    pl
Blanchard, Jos W    p mill op
    Lela C (Ray    ho
Bonney, G H    eng
    Bertha E (Doten    ho
    Timothy D    pl
    Gladys E    pl
Bouchard, Joseph    lab
    —— (St Pierre    ho

| | | | |
|---|---|---|---|
| Elmira | pl | Kenneth | |
| Selbena | pl | Brown, Claude F | mill op |
| Bradeen, John N | | Gertrude E (Watson | ho |
| *Lulu P (m Glover R Falls | | Albert C | |
| Myra P (Bailey | ho | Brown, S R | lab |
| Everett I | stu | Cora G (Kilgore | ho |
| Myrtle A | pl | Eva B | pl |
| Bradeen, B V | mill op | Frank M | |
| Bradeen, Seth B far Frye | | Ethan W | |
| Laura A (Hutchinson | ho | Brown, Harriet C (Wilson Dix | |
| Ethel A | ho | *Geo J s mkr · Dix | |
| Lester A | pl | Bryanton, Kenneth M mill op | |
| Bradeen, Arthur W R R ser | | Annie M (Haines | ho |
| Ethel H (Bixby | ho | Buckman, John C | car |
| Brenick, John | lab | Sarah F (Richardson | ho |
| Sarah E (Hudson | ho | *Clara A (m Mitchell | ho |
| John J | pl | | Roxbury |
| Mary | pl | Edith E (m Dorr | ho |
| Helena A | pl | *Addie B (m Philbrick | ho |
| Lawrence H | | Dix Ctr, No 1 | |
| Brown, Vesta A (Cooper | | Bumbus, Samuel H lab Rid | |
| *Sarah E (m Holbroke ho | | Cedora J (Andrews | ho |
| Plymouth | | Burgess, A S grain dlr Rid | |
| *Addie M (m Wheeler | ho | Rose A (Wing | ho |
| Waterville | | Leon L | eng |
| *Chas W lab Winterport | | *Ismay L (m Downs | |
| *Carrie M (m Smith | | | R Falls |
| Stockton Springs | | Leona | pl |
| Brown, Ernest A | mill op | Burgess, Wm O far Rid | |
| Josephine E (Lapiere | ho | Annie A (Frost | ho |
| Linwood J | | Burley, Nettie G bag mill Rid | |
| Brown, Joseph | mill op | Burns, P F s mason Rid | |
| Laura (McWhinney | ho | Joan (—— | ho |
| Sherley | | Lizzie I (m Oldham | ho |

| | | | |
|---|---|---|---|
| Macie S | mill op | .Florence C (Eastman | ho |
| John R | mill op | Janet M | |
| Margaret | mill op | Carey, Mark | mill op |
| Peter L | mill op | Ellen (Blacquar | ho |
| Grace E | stu | Martha | pl |
| Burrows, Robt | car | Lena | pl |
| Margaret (Law | ho | Wilson | pl |
| Infant | | Ellen | pl |
| Bushey, Joseph | Rid | Mark | |
| Clara (Sousie | ho | Carkhan, H B  far | |
| Bushey, Perley  lab | Rid | Annie (Welch | ho |
| Nellie (Bishop | ho | Madge E | |
| Perley J | | Carr, Elbridge | far |
| Bushley, Nelson | lab | Carver, Edwin H | |
| Mary (Roolo | ho | ptr & paper hgr | Rid |
| Annie | stenog | Sadie M (Howard | ho |
| Bushie, Lena | pl | Winnie M | pl |
| Butterfield, M E  mach | Rid | Lena E | pl |
| Clara A (Richards | ho | Wesley H | |
| Buzzell, Lovina E (Howard | | Carville, E L  mill op | Rid |
| | Rid | Gertrude A (Thornton | ho |
| Elmer G | pl | Walter L | pl |
| Buzzell, Wm E  s mason | Rid | Bernard E | |
| | | Casey, F B  millwright | Rid |
| C | | Mary H (Sutton | ho |
| | | Pearle W | |
| Campbell, Joshua L  car | Hale | Donald C | |
| Millie C (Coffran | ho | Casey, J J  mill op | Rid |
| Elna A | stu | Lillian S (Mitchell | ho |
| Freda N | pl | Chabot, E  mill op | R Falls |
| Gladys J | pl | Zelley (Richard | ho |
| Millie A | pl | George | |
| Horatio N | | Chase, Henry  far | Dix |
| Campbell, Clarence E lab Hale | | -  Martha A (Wade | ho |

| | | | |
|---|---|---|---|
| Kate J (m Flagg | ho | Cole, T Percy | mach |
| Zenas B | far | Mary L (Lagrange | ho |
| Ida M (m Howard | ho | Harlon L | |
| *Fannie L (m Blaisdell | | Cole, Chas E lumb | Rid |
| East Dix | | Albertha S (Daggett | ho |
| Checkley, Margaret mill op | | Fred | lab |
| Checkley, Agnes | pl | Effie M | stu |
| Cheney, Ben mill op | | Manley W | stu |
| Delia (Laclair | ho | Cole, Frances D bag mill | Rid |
| Manda | pl | Collins, A J mill op | Rid |
| Eva | pl | Iola G (Long | ho |
| Ben Jr | pl | Collins, Donald fire | Rid |
| O Villa | | Collins, B J millwright | |
| Childs, H A s mkr | Dix | Jennie (McInnis | ho |
| Rose M (Gilman | ho | Helen M | |
| Fred H | stu | Conway, Micheal R steam fit | |
| Martha E | pl | Maggie (Sutton | ho |
| Childs, P E s mkr | Dix | Helena M | pl |
| Florence M (Lamb | ho | James A | |
| Elwin C | pl | Viola M | |
| Clifford E | | Corner, Philip mill op | |
| Clark, John F | car | Olive (Myer | ho |
| Mary E (Russell | ho | Plessie | |
| Clements, E E mill op | Rid | Joseph | |
| Myra B (Spaulding | ho | Napoleon | |
| Bernie I | | Peter | |
| Clifford, Chas A bk kpr | Rid | Corner, Chas fireman | Park |
| Lawrence A | pl | Gulinn (Bourk | ho |
| Philip A | pl | Agnes M | pl |
| Carlton H | pl | Anna | |
| Charles H | pl | Cotie, Napoleon | mill op |
| Maud I (Blanchard | ho | Rose (Lavoie | ho |
| Gladys B | pl | Mary L | mill op |
| Clinch, Henry retd | Rid | Rose A | mill op |

| | | |
|---|---|---|
| Emile | mill op | |
| Emily | pl | |
| Omer | pl | |
| H—— | pl | |
| Couture, Archille | mill op | |
| Delphine (Daigle | ho | |
| Crowell,—— | | |
| Information withheld | | |
| Crummett, Wilber S  P M  Rid | | |
| Linnie M (Taylor | ho | |
| Earl E | pl | |
| Curran, Patrick | fireman | |
| Annie (Curran | ho | |
| Nicholas | pl | |
| Morton | pl | |
| Annie M | | |
| Lawrence | | |

**D**

| | | |
|---|---|---|
| Daggett, O H | mill op | Rid |
| Daggett, F R | mill op | Rid |
| Daley, Selden N | ptr | Rid |
| Nellie E (Knapp | ho | |
| Pearle M | pl | |
| Davenport, E A | | |
| ptr & paper hgr | | |
| Alice V (Gould | ho | |
| Verona A | pl | |
| Rena R | pl | |
| Ardel R | | |
| Davenport, Dennis M | ptr | |
| Elbert A | ptr | |
| Myrtie L (m Haynes | ho | |

| | | |
|---|---|---|
| Davis, Wm H | mill op | Rid |
| Florence M (Ames | | ho |
| Earl C | | pl |
| Chester H | | pl |
| Davis, A E | mer | Rid |
| Annie C (Johnson | | ho |
| Claud A | | pl |
| A Mabel | | pl |
| Day, Lois A (Curtis | | Rid |
| Allison L | | car |
| Clarence W | | ptr |
| Georgia A | | pl |
| Dean, Alex | lab | Rid |
| Lizzie (Legeer | | ho |
| Angie | | pl |
| Ada | | pl |
| Anthony | | pl |
| Charlotte | | |
| Desire | | |
| Decker, E A | p mill op | Rid |
| Ella M (Kneeland | | ho |
| Oren E | | stu |
| Nellie M | | stu |
| Arthur L | | pl |
| Lillian P | | pl |
| Raymond A | | pl |
| Decker, Pheba A (Gordon | | ho |
| Edgar A | mill op | |
| *Josephine M (m Nason | | |
| No Waterford | | |
| *Everett E far Kent's Hill | | |
| *Stephen V | far | |
| South Waterford | | |
| *Roscoe R | Millinocket | |

| | | | | | |
|---|---|---|---|---|---|
| Decker, John O | mill op | Dorr, Lottie A | ho | Rid |
| Georgia A (Dyer | | Dowling, James | | far |
| Dikes, Chas mill op | Rid | Elizabeth S (Luter | | ho |
| Donnell, W A | car | George E | | car |
| Bell F (Frost | ho | Mary E (m Wood | | ho |
| Raymond W | | Dowling, George E | | car |
| Dorothy, John | mill op | Cathrine R (Hobin | | ho |
| Mary (Wedge | ho | Lizzie J | | stu |
| Lillie (m Dorothy | ho | Hazel M | | pl |
| Dorothy, P C | mill op | Marion J | | pl |
| Lillie (Chase | ho | Doyen, Chas mill op | | Rid |
| Beatrice M | pl | Doyen, J M | | Rid |
| Blanche S | | constable, mer & far | | |
| Lucy L | | Angie S (Haines | | ho |
| Dorr, Samuel S | far | Bert G | | lab |
| Clara C (Harlow | ho | Bernard M | | lab |
| George A | mill op | Perle A | | pl |
| Challotte A (m Kimball | | Mertie A | | pl |
| *Orissa M (m Reckford | | Drake, Geo H box shop | | Rid |
| | Dix | Jennie M (Maxwell | | ho |
| Charles E | lab | Dresser, Ecla | | mill op |
| *Florilla (m Worthley ho | | Driscol, Dennis | | mill op |
| | Berry Mills | Agnes (Foley | | ho |
| *Martha J (m Wyman | | Droin, Joseph | | mill op |
| | No Woodstock, N H | Emma (Pullin | | ho |
| Elizabeth M (m Whitman | | Philip | | mill op |
| Dorr, Jarvis M | lab | Berard | | mill op |
| Samuel W | | Alphonse | | team |
| Dorr, S O | car | Leah (m Ralduc | | ho |
| *Minnie E (m Farrer | ho | Duley, F A | | Rid |
| | So Paris | plumber & steam fit | | |
| *Eugene H cl So Paris | | Lizzie E (Wills | | ho |
| Edith E (Buckman | ho | Harold W | | pl |
| Clyde H | pl | Flora E | | pl |

Harry A
Dunn, L J     mill op     Rid
    Mary A (C——     ho
    Agnes F
Dunphy, N T     mill op
    Maud B (Childs     ho
Durgin, Frank A   toll kpr   Rid
Durgin, Bessie M    cl    Rid
Dwyer, W T    steam fit    Rid
    Mary A
    William R

## E

Eastman, Willard   far   Hale
    Angenett (Flagg     ho
    Lilla A (m Weeks     ho
    Arthur R     lab
    Florence P (m Campbell
Eastman, W O   blk & car   Dix
    Ava I (Howard     ho
Eaton, Chas     Auctioneer
Edes, Eliza (Williams     ho
    Fred H     mill op
    *Rosaline(m Gardner   N Y
    Willie     mill op
    Charles J     pl
Edson, F C   p mill op   Rid
    Lydia E (Mayo     ho
Eliott, B W     far
    Maria A (Lufkin     ho
    *Jennie L (m White     ho
    *Dwight D   far   Monmouth
Ellingwood, Hollis J     guide

Grace L (Haskell     ho
Ellingwood, H E    mer    Rid
    *Aked D     printer
      Milan, N H
    Roland P     mer
    *Minnie E     tr
      Goffstown, N H
    *Gertrude E(m Fogg
      West Milan, N H
    *Edgar E     cook
      West Milan, N H
    *Frank P   barber   R Falls
    M Huldah(Huntly   dr mkr
Emery, Wm A    master mech
        Rid
    Ida M (Andrews     ho
    William F
Emery, Ellen B (Andrews
    William J     bk kpr
    Arthur L     lab
    Jesse J     hostler
Ethridge, Harry E    fireman
    Helena C (Kilgore     ho
    Florence E
Ethridge, N W     millwright
    Juda M (Glines     ho
    Harry E     fireman

## F

Farland, Alfred   p mill   Rid
    Mary (——     ho
    Flora (m Muise     ho
    Lora     bag mill op

| | | | |
|---|---|---|---|
| Arthur | pl | Fisher, E F    lab | Rid |
| Cora | pl | Jennie P (Bennett | ho |
| Alphonse | pl | Myrtie E | pl |
| Albert | | Glenna M | pl |
| Alvina | | Edwin F Jr | pl |
| Farrington, Abel Jr | Rid | Nellie M | |
| *Sadie E    table girl | | Rosanna M | |
| Mechanic Falls | | Fitzgerald, J P    car | Rid |
| *Lea A (m —— | ho | Maud L (Burley | ho |
| No 1, Dix | | Carrie C | |
| Gerald | pl | Fitzpatrick, Wm    truckman | |
| Clara E (Whitney | ho | | Rid |
| Windsor | | Lena M (Dugee | ho |
| Farrington, Abel    far | Dix | Gladys | pl |
| Ellen F C (Witham | ho | Flagg, John    lab | Rid |
| *Chas W    s mill op | Dix | William    lab | |
| *Emily F (m Burgess | ho | Ida | ho |
| R F D, R Falls | | *Flagg, Eugene    lab | |
| *Henry E    far, ptr & blk | | Berry Mills | |
| West Bridgton | | Carrie E (Taylor | Rid |
| *Susan E (m Holman | ho | William M | pl |
| No 1, Dix | | Victor E | pl |
| Filiult, P J    mill op | Rid | Flagg, Mary W (Kelley | Rid |
| Mary C (Robarge | ho | Eugene    river driver | |
| Ora G | mill op | *Ronello    far    Bethel | |
| John B | mill op | *Wm D    lab    Wilton | |
| Mary L | pl | Flagg, Geo H    far    Hale | |
| Wilfred F | pl | Katie J (Chase | ho |
| Margaret C | pl | Flaherty, Coleman    fireman | |
| Loretta G | | Mary (Curran | ho |
| Irene | | Margaret | pl |
| Fisher, J G    Cong clerg | Rid | Mary | pl |
| Agnes (Waugh | ho | Annie | pl |
| R Edgar | pl | Patrick | pl |

Katie
Martin
John
Fogg, A E     car     Rid
   Ora A (Lovejoy     ho
   *Carrie G (in Merrill
                 R Falls
   Edwin A     pl
Foley, J F     mach
   Clara A (Bennett     ho
Fornier, Jos   p mill op    Rid
   Sophrony (Baker     ho
   Arthur     pl
   William     pl
   Alsilde     pl
   Lena     pl
Ford, George C    mason    Rid
   Lizzie M (Goddard     ho
Foy, A S     mill op
   Minnie (Nelson     ho
   Mabel A
Fraser, J E     far
   Mary E (Hunnewell     ho
Fraser, David M     far
Frecker, Johanna (Moore   Rid
   Arthur W     mech
Frost, Dan'l G     far
   Imogene M (Hall     ho
Frost, Chas A    R R ser    Dix
   Minnie M (Kennison     ho
   Percy A     pl
*Frost, Mary L     nurse
   John Hopkins Hospital
       Baltimore, Md

Fuller, Geo E     butcher
          Whitmanville
   Florence (Johnson     ho
   Sion E
Furbush, Fred     car
   Catherine L (Moore     ho
   Frederick J     pl
   Hazel G     pl
   Clarence W     pl
   Fern L     pl
   Olive F
Ferguson, Wm C   saw filer   Rid

### G

Gagne, Geo A    steam fit    Rid
   Bertha (——     ho
   Albert     pl
   Ronald
   Lillian
Gallant, Jos     s mason
   Georgia A (Dupill     ho
   Alma (m Sheehan     ho
   E——     lab
   Adella
   Edgar
   Edwin
*Gallop, Julian     far
   Verna R (Richards     ho
   Doris E
   Myron E
Gammon, V P    R R ser    Rid
   Sibyl A (Barrett     ho
Garcelon, Chas     mach

| | | | |
|---|---|---|---|
| May J (Stewart | ho | *Herbert O far | Phillips |
| V L | ho | Mary M (Mosher | ho |
| Doris G | | Gleason, F P | mill op |
| Garno, Fred team | Rid | Gertrude M (Seberling | ho |
| Melvina (Lahay | ho | Wallace F | stu |
| Jennie | pl | Emma Gertrude | |
| Emma | pl | Goff, Albion K far | Hale |
| Annie | pl | Annett W (Storer | ho |
| Fred | | Eugene H | team |
| Gilchrist, F H cl | Rid | Guy H | lab |
| Minnie S (Virgin | ho | James | stu |
| Ethel L | pl | Lucy J | pl |
| Edith A | pl | Goodrich, J F far | Rid |
| Vergina A | | Goodrich, C F far | Rid |
| Gill, Richard mill op | Rid | Mary J (Proctor | ho |
| Rachel (Turple | ho | Harry F | lab |
| Glenroy | pl | Goodwin, E P mer | Rid |
| Sherley E | | Nancy W (Wyman | ho |
| Sherwood A | | Goodwin, W W mer | Rid |
| Gille, Lena | ho | Ella A (Berry | ho |
| Given, Warren A blk | Hale | *Mary D (m Butterfield | |
| Rebecca J (Briney | ho | | East Dix |
| Gleason, E H | law | Berton W | |
| Mary E (Crowell | ho | | plumber & heater |
| Basil C | pl | Gordon, B S p mill | Rid |
| Elsie M | | Florence J (Wing | ho |
| Gleason, Geo H | far | Alfred L | |
| Elizabeth (Kimball | ho | Graffam, Wm | far |
| Gleason, Archie A milkman | | *Edw W | R Falls |
| Nona B (Packard | ho | *Lizzie M (m Morse | ho |
| Lena F | pl | | Steep Falls |
| Richard P | | *Jennie D (m Jordan | ho |
| Gleason, D O | far | | High, So Paris |
| Enna L (m Parks | ho | | |

*Frank J        lawn tender
                      R Falls
Groven, Jos      bag mill   Rid
    Mary B (Demais          ho
    *Josie (m Hasie    R Falls
    Joseph A            lab
    Rosie           bag mill op
    Jennie          bag mill op
    Mary            bag mill op
    Mildred                 pl
    Abbie                   pl
    Alfred                  pl
    Leona
Guilda, J B      p mill op   Rid
    Elizabeth R (Moody       ho


                **H**

Hackett, John J        mill op
    Laura M (Harrington  ho
Haines, II J         steam fit
    Rose E (Virgin          ho
    Virgil H
Haines, Caroline A (——   ho
    Edward             mill op
    Lulu L (m Harlow       ho
    Myrtie E (m Dorington ho
Haldane, Frank   fireman  Rid
    Elizabeth (Bradshaw     ho
    Jessie                  pl
    Robert
    Infant
Hall, Wm F         car     Rid
    Nellie A (Curtis        ho

George W                   far
    Lida S                  pl
    Leslie F                pl
Hall, Zenas W            retd
    Linnie M (Verrill       ho
    *Zina G pl Auburn, No 4
    Agnes M                 pl
    H Margaret              pl
Hall, John iron moulder  Rid
    Margaret (Neil          ho
    Mabel M
    Hazel N
Hammond, Ella D    ho   Rid
Hammond, Vera M    pl   Rid
Hanley, Thos A    sales  Rid
    Mabel T (Towne
    Gladys                  pl
    William T               pl
Hanlon, O L  phy & sur  Rid
    Mildred B (Woodward  ho
    Francis W
Harkness, E T  p mill op  Rid
    Flora M (Ryan          ho
    Everett                 pl
Harlow, Henry W    far   Dix
    Affie (Holman          ho
    *Henry H           piping
               Hartford, Conn
    Elbridge M        t p mill
    Anna                    pl
    Neal                    pl
    Maynard                 pl
    Hildred                 pl
    Amasa                   pl

Helen
Infant
Harlow, Nettie F (Goding
　　　　　　　　　dr mkr
　Harold L　　　　　　cl
　Eva F (m Toothaker　ho
　George M　　　　　　stu
Harlow, Harold L　　　cl
　Lulu L (Haines　　　ho
　Bernice L
　Doris A
Harmon, Chas J　phy & sur
　　　　　　　　　　Rid
　Rosamon L (Burgess　ho
Haskell, Amorena P　dr mkr
Hatch, Helen E　ho　Frye
Hayes, Mary A (Durgin　Rid
Haynes, Hugh　　　mill op
　Joanna (Frecker　　ho
　Benedict　　　　　　pl
　Hugh R　　　　　　pl
　Elvina C　　　　　　pl
Haynes, Leon　　　　car
　Myrtie L (Davenport
Healey, Wm F　mill op　Rid
　Laura E (McInnis　　ho
　John D
Henry, Osmond J　　　ptr
　Katie R (Riley　　　ho
　Gerald W
　Annie May
Herrick, Ruth E　pl　R Falls
Herrick, Frank A　mill boss
　Emily C (Fessenden　ho

Marriner F　　　　　pl
Hewison, Wm　mill op　Rid
　Harriett (Dikes　　ho
Hicks, Warren J　p mill　Rid
　Cora J (Long　　　ho
　Beulah I
　Daisy L
Holland, J M　trav sales　Dix
　M E (Newman　　　ho
　Minnie M　　　P O Asst
　*John M (Grocer
　　　　　　　So Rumford
Holland, Edw T　far　R Falls
　Lillian (Abbott　　ho
Horn, Vivian C　far　Dix
　Betsey M (Trask　　ho
Holt, H A　　ret'd　　Rid
Holt, Henry T　　stg driver
　　　　　　　　　　Rid
　Abbie M (Whitman　ho
Holt, Ezra A　pl　　Hale
Houghton, Lydia E (Cushman
　*Elizabeth M　tr　Wilton
　*Cyrus G　drover　Wilton
Howard, Lewis D　　　car
　Mary A (Richards　　ho
　Daniel J　　　　　　pl
Howard, Bert I　far　Rid
　Etta G (Babb　　　ho
　Willie F　　　　　　far
　Albert W　　　　　　pl
　Agnes G　　　　　　pl
　Clarence I　　　　　pl
Howard, A F　far　R Falls

| | | | |
|---|---|---|---|
| Bert I | far | *Fred S | s mkr |
| A F | far | | Haverhill, Mass |
| Chas J | far | *Chas D | s mkr |
| Ida M (Chase | ho | | Haverhill, Mass |
| Howard, A F | far | Lewis D | car |
| Effie I (Burgess | ho | *Catherine (in Googin |
| Nellie H | pl | | Portland |
| Willard A | pl | *Ida M | clerk |
| Elwood E | pl | 239 Congress, Portland |
| Cliffie L | | Howard, L A | ptr | Rid |
| Lena E | | Nellie E (Marston | ho |
| Howard, O M | far | Dix | Sherwin R |
| Ava I (m Eastman | ho | Huston, Clark | blk |
| *Walter E | car | Dix | Annie (——— | ho |
| *Arno G | far | No 1 Dix | Huston, Anna L (Glines | ho |
| *M Treat | s mill op | Dix | Huston, Louie C | pl |
| *Herbert C | s mill op | Dix |
| Hutcheon, A | ir moulder | Rid |
| Jennie C (Gibson | ho |
| Richard G | lab | Isbaster, Lorin F | eng | Rid |
| Nellie R | pl | Agnes E | ho |
| William R | pl | David H | eng |
| Ethel E | pl | *J Walter | mech | Rockland |
| Martha M | pl |
| Hutchinson, Wm | team | Rid |
| Howard, Gladys F | stu | Rid |
| Howard, J L | opera ho | Rid | James, Armour | eng |
| Jennie M (Lovejoy | ho | Sarah E (Dunn | ho |
| Fred I | pl | Florence M | pl |
| Howard, Chas I | ret'd | Rid | James W | pl |
| Sarah A (Ludden | ho | Jones, Howard C | far | R Falls |
| John L | trial justice | Jordan, Carl C | billing cl | Rid |
| Sadie M (m Carver | ho | Catherine L (Bolton | ho |
| Howard, C L | cont & bldr | Rid | Alice E |

J

## K

Keenan, J W   Ber M Co   Rid
  Esther C (McLaughlin   ho
  Helen A   pl
  John H   pl
  Mary T
  Alban J
Keene, Emily H (Hayes   Rid
  E Louise   pl
Keenan, Lewis   scaler   Rid
  Alice (McLaughlin   ho
Kelley, Mary W (Burgess   Rid
  Edward A   lab
Kelley, Wm H   mach   Rid
  Winona (Barton   milliner
  Vere W   stu
  Linwood V   stu
Kempton, Chester   car
  May S (Hinckley   ho
  Clara M
Kennard, W G   st cutter   Rid
  Almira B (Sargent   ho
  *Maud E (m Nutter   ho
            Maplewood
  Annie M   ·   mill op
  Flossie B   mill op
  Archie H   pl
  Chas O   pl
  Leslie E
Kershan, Bertram   mill op
  Etta (McCurdy   ho
  Bertram G
Keys, Chas S   scaler & cl   Rid

  Mabel F (Hewey   ho
  Chas II
  Marie T
Kidder, Adelbert   retd
  Addie E (Gleason   ho
  *Lena A (m White
            Springfield, Ill
  Josephine L   ho
  Helen E (m Smith   ho
  Grace L   ho
  *Eugene O   car   R Falls
  *Arthur D   car   R Falls
Kidder, R A   far   Hale
  Anna R (Reed   ho
  Louise M   cl
  Delia A   pub ho
  John F   stu
  R W   pl
Kidder, Lydia H (Holman   Dix
  Fred W   team
  Alfred H   pl
  Wilfred   pl
Kidder, Josie L   ho   Dix
Kidder, Sarah G (Furness   ho
  Delbert   retd
  *Geo D   car   R Falls
  Freemont   far   Dix
Kimball, Lottie A (——   Rid
  Mabel L (m Smith   ho
  Martha G   pl
  Irving B   pl
  Clara A   pl
Knauer, Jno   mill op   Rid
  Barbara (Beller   ho

Mamie mill op
Willie mill op
John mill op
Annie pl
Lizzie pl
Rosie pl
Charlie pl
Barbara
Eva
Knightly, H  bd sawyer  Rid
Ella J (Swett  ho
Knowlton, Arthur A  pl  Rid
Knowlton, W W
Elvira E (Walker  ho
Leonard I  lumb
Knox, Chester L  car  Rid
Flavilla A (Whitman  ho
Danville I  cl
Susie M  mill op

L

Ladd, Sarah H (——  ho
Warren H  far
Willis R  far
*Jno R  ,  far & cream col
Roxbury
Emma F (m Hannaford
Nancy E (m Richards  ho
*Forest W  far  Rum Point
Jesse A  lab
*Lucinda M  comb shop
Attleboro, Mass
Fred L  pl

Cleveland  pl
Lageer, M F  saloon  Rid
Charlotte (Lageer  ho
Alice (m Dane  ho
Lageer, Frank F  lab  Rid
Dena (Poral  ho
Fred P  mill op
*Lillie (m Michaud  ho
West Enfield
Jennie B  bag mill
Eva M  bag mill
Philip  pl
Helen  pl
Fred  pl
George
Emma
Lamb, Martilla A (Lamb  Dix
*Frank A  car  Dix
*Fred J  fore liv stable
334 Fourth, So Boston
Scott A  t p mill
Florence M (m Childs  ho
Lambart, Carrie H (Lane  ho
Irvin D  lumb
Lang, A J  eng
*Geo F  mer Boston, Mass
28 A Huntington Ave
*Arthur L  barber
Andover
*Ethel C  188 Hillside
Roxbury, Mass
Cyntha S (Barrett  ho
Christena E  pl
Law, Duncan  mill op

| | | | |
|---|---|---|---|
| Mary (Bruce | ho | Lizzie | |
| Margaret (m Burrows | ho | Mabel | |
| Martha | pl | Idella | |
| Robert | pl | Maloon, N J | |
| Leavitt, F H far | Dix | Carrie H (Lambert | ho |
| Leavitt, C E mill op | Rid | Vinie M (m Vaughan | |
| Nellie (Gardiner | ho | Beulah P | pl |
| Lebarron, H E blk | Rid | Martinson, Anna (Wiken | Rid |
| Mabel M (Foss | ho | R (m Anderson | ho |
| *Lena A (m Blanchard | | *Martin boss in Mill | |
| R Falls | | Gorham, N H | |
| C Everett mill op | | Marston, Nellie E (Knapp | Rid |
| Leckey, G W mill op | Rid | Edith M mill op | |
| Nellie M (Chadbourne | ho | Marston, W L eng & far | |
| Wirt | | R Falls | |
| Libby, Chas A p mill | Rid | Georgia A (Monk | ho |
| Long, Cora J (Harriman | Rid | Ethel G | ho |
| Iola G (m Collins | ho | Ernest | |
| Lila N | ho | Leon W | |
| Jennie A | pl | Harry L | |
| John A | pl | Henry | |
| | | Martin, Chas G mach | |
| **M** | | Clara M (Beauprey | ho |
| | | Celia D | pl |
| Macewen, Horace millwright | | Alfred W | |
| Rid | | Maud L | |
| May (Matthewson | | George A | |
| Mary E | | Mason, J P team R Falls | |
| Margaret E | | Annie O (Otis | ho |
| Robert C | | Hazel R | |
| Madison, Annie S (Myers | | Mason, Ansel L team | Rid |
| James W | mill wk | Mason, Ida M ho | Rid |
| Alma G | mill wk | Mason, I W | |
| Jos E | mill wk | lumb mill mfg & law | |

| | | | |
|---|---|---|---|
| Winnie E (Wheeler | ho | Kate M | pl |
| Mayers, Nicholas | lab | Nina M | pl |
| Sider (Labishaw | ho | McDonald, Herbert J car | Rid |
| Mary | | Alice C (Crawford | ho |
| Geneva | | *Saml G meat cutter | |
| Gladys | | 155 Federal, Portland | |
| McCaffrty, Hugh meat dlr | | *Maud A (m Christopher | |
| Flora J (Jenkins | ho | Pejepscot | |
| Robert T | | Robert C | lab |
| McCleod, Mathew fore mill yd | | *Herbert W bell boy | |
| | Rid | Lewiston | |
| Clara M (Littlefield | ho | Florence C | pl |
| C Roy | pl | Hazel M F | pl |
| Inez M | pl | Henry E M | pl |
| Geneva M | pl | Leora E | |
| Mathew C | | Douglass H | |
| Cecil L | | McInism, Norman mill op Rid | |
| McCollister, L H scaler | Rid | Lorinda (McCray | ho |
| Carrie M (Record | ho | Hazel May | pl |
| McCrea, P H millwright | | Grace F | pl |
| Maude L (Greene | ho | William A | |
| Catherine | pl | Mildred L | |
| Dorothy | | McIntyre, Maurice bdg ho Dix | |
| McCray, Angus millwright | | Nancy C (Martin | ho |
| | Rid | Ina A t p mill op | |
| Lydia M (Leslie | ho | Adelbert D | team |
| Viola M | pl | J Alfred | stu |
| Florence E | | Maurice M | pl |
| McDonald, John p mill | Rid | McLaughlin, Jas T | eng |
| Christie (McDougass | | Mary O (Withee | ho |
| Angus A | | Annie E | pl |
| McDonald, Ronald mill op | | McLean, Della S (Ames | Rid |
| | Rid | McNaught, Miss —— | |
| Mary M (—— | ho | McNeil, Jno | lab |

Bella (Bateman ho    Catherine E
Margaret E ho | Morton, Ira P    R R ser
William J pl | Moulton, L F   car   R Falls
Anna B pl |    Gertrude M (Bowdoin ho
Edw H pl | Murch, H C   mill op   Rid
H D pl |    Blanche A (Damon ho
Clayton |    Esther B
Eva V |    Olive M
McWhinney, Fred   mill op | M——, Peter   lab   Rid
Merchant, S G   far   Hale |    Flora M (Ferland ho
   Nellie M (Sargent ho |    Mary L
Mills, C W   steam fit & piper |    Peter Jr
           Rid | Myre, Patrick
   Annie B (Gille ho | Myshrall, Perley M mech Rid
Mills, Arthur H   mill op   Rid |    Lilla M (Rankin ho
   Almeda (Gille ho |    Irene A
Mitchell, A L   team   Rid |
   Josephine J (Emery ho |            N
   Lillian S (m C—— ho |
   Alice M pl | Newman, Myrtilla H (Zetten
Mitchell, Milo   far   Hale |            Dix
   Ora M (Edmunds ho |    Madana E (m Holland ho
   Merton W pl |    *Zuedo L (m Stanley   ho
   Ray E |        Roxbury, Mass
Moody, Henry   mill op | Newton, Geo W   mill op
   Florinda (Ashmore ho |    *Geo W Jr   Newport
   Joseph pl |    *Ellen E (m Moore
Morris, Mary A (Richards Rid |        Newport
   *Adelbert M   far   Leeds |    *Frank B   stu   Lewiston
Morris, Fred L   p mill | Nichols, Geo M   car & sawyer
   Annie M (Rose ho |            Rid
   Morrison, Dan'l   fireman |    Nettie F (Brown ho
   Catherine (Grimley ho |    Bernard M
   Nicholas G | Niles, M L   cond R R

Minnie (Berry ho
Boutelle
Nugas, Jno p mill Rid
Ola V (Ogee ho
Elsie pl
Marion
Josie

## O

Oldham, Perry Mill op Rid
Lizzie (Burns ho
Otis, Lydia O (Russell R Falls
Ovila, L piper
Amelia (Laclair ho
Ougee, Jos mill hand Rid
Delia (Asslin ho
Eva M
Elsie M
Ougee, Jos p mill Rid
E—— (Canstand ho
Lena M (m Fitzpatrick
Ola V (m Nogus ho
Rosa ho
Fred pl
Philip pl

## P

Packard, Archer eng Rid
Emily (Neal ho
Hazel M pl
Elois N pl
Paine, Jos D mill Rid

Olivia E (Richardson ho
Palmer, A D mill op Rid
Palmer, Geo W car Rid
Florence E (Weaver ho
Park, Henry W mer & P M
*Albert D So Paris
reg Probate, Oxford Co
Etta P (m Richards tr
*Ellery C lawyer Bethel
Enna L (Gleason ho
Helena O (m Small ho
*Lucy E (m Moore R Falls
Henry W Jr mer
Eva Grace cl
Pelletier, Frank lab
Delima (Sager ho
Rose ho
Jennie (m Chabot
*Frank switchman
Boston, Mass
Alex mill op
Penaley, Thos W
Frances M (Swett ho
Perkins, Sarah E ho
Perkins, S L ho
Perkins, F A ptr & dep sher
Claude A ptr
*Nellie M (m Caldwell ho
E Andover
Eula D mill op
Retha F pl
Rose E (Whitman ho
Perry, Willie C mach Rid
Mary C (Smith ho

| | | | |
|---|---|---|---|
| Jasper C | mach | Chas S | ptr |
| Jesse W | lab | Mildreth F | ho |
| Almon E | pl | | |
| Victor M | pl | **Q** | |
| Perry, Philip | ptr | Quigg, Jas T | mach |
| Victoria (Arsenault | ho | Margaret A (Kelley | ho |
| Eddie | pl | Geo F | mill op |
| Perry, P | fireman | Willis M | |
| Maggie (Gallant | ho | Quinn, David | elec |
| Pheba | mill op | Florence M (Coyle | ho |
| Phil | mill op | | |
| Anthony | mill op | **R** | |
| John | pl | Ramsdy, D S ho | Rid |
| Lena | pl | Lillian I (Bishop | ho |
| Madeline | pl | Rankin, Edw R millwright | |
| Archie | pl | | Rid |
| Peter | | Ella V (Warren | ho |
| Paul | | Lilla M (m Mishrall | ho |
| Plant, Amos mill op R Falls | | Joseph W | stu |
| Plummer, Chas A | millman | Reed, Abbie S (Landers | ho |
| | Rid | Mary L | stu |
| *Ida (m Peavy New York | | Martha S (m Spaulding | |
| Poulin, Wm | lab | Carrie S (m Varney | ho |
| Pratt, Wm N | ice | Elma L | stu |
| Frances S (Penley | | Reed, S A mer & far | Frye |
| Clara E , | pl | Sarah W (Judkins | ho |
| Gladys M | pl | *Geo B | fore mill |
| Esther E | pl | W Milan, N H | |
| Iva May | | Allen J | tr |
| Richard Stevens | | John S | stu |
| Proctor, C W (Morey | ho | Sila G | ho & tr |
| May J (m Goodrich | ho | Regar, John J | Rid |
| *Addie (m Holt Andover | | Rich, Elwin blk | Rid |
| *Lillian W (m Wyman ho | | Clara E (Russ | ho |
| 63 Sagamore, Chelsea, Mass | | | |

Richards, Wilson    mill op
   Sarah A (Monaghan    ho
   Lena B    pl
   Eliza E    pl
   William F    pl
   Wilson A
   George A
Richards, Elizabeth L
      (Barnard
   Samuel D    far
   *Chas B    liv & mer
     Cando, No Dakota
   Hiram T  wood, coal & ice
   Mary R (m Howard    ho
   Vena R (m Gallop    ho
   *Hannah P    office wk
  200 Phenix bldg, Mina, Minn
Richards, Samuel D    far
   Jennie (Stora    ho
Richards, H T coal, wood & ice
   Florence L (Thomas    ho
Richards, A L    mason    Rid
   Ella L (Lambert    ho
   Mildred F
Richards, Philip    car    Rid
   Lizzie (Landrie    ho
   Mary E    mill op
   Edmond    pl
   Philip    pl
   Alice
   Margaret
Richards, Alonzo    car    Rid
   Nellie E (Wellman    ho
   Clarence A    pl

   Ralph    pl
   Raymond M    pl
Richards, Jos  box shop    Rid
   Mary M (Perry    ho
   Tom J    pl
   Mary J    pl
   John G    pl
   Alfred A    pl
   Willie F
   Elizabeth Ann
   Mary Jane
Richards, Lucy S (Allen    ho
   C V    team
Richards, C V    team    Rid
   Nancy E (Ladd    ho
   L Ethel    pl
   S Evelyn    pl
Richards, F A  mill man    Rid
   Hattie A (Swain    ho
   Elva A    pl
   L Helena    pl
   Vilda F    pl
   F Minard    pl
   Harold F
Richardson, Olesia E (Bodwell
        Rid
   *Edw E    elec moterman
      Scarboro
   *Albert A    grocer
   317 Congress, Portland
Robarge, Adeline (Robarge
   Mary C (m Filliault    ho
   *Ceduli (m Beliveau
       R Falls

*Fred ice man Lewiston
*Geo O bleachery
Lewiston
Roberts, D F far Rid
Lizzie H (Trask ho
S Wm R R ser
Mary E ho
Lydia H pl
Amos W pl
Robbins, C S barber Rid
Ella (Hood ho
Roberts, Alfred E agt tea Co
Margaret A (Woodworth
Hartley F pl
Olive M pl
L W pl
Laura B pl
Rodgerson, David millwright
Helen N (Babb ho
Ada R pl
Ethel R
Rose, A P p mill Rid
Florence M (Libby
Gerald A pl
Rounds, G B stone mason
Rid
Nellie E (Kennard ho
Osburn G lab
Guy pl
Eva M pl
Infant
Roy, Theofiele meat cut
R Falls
Josephine (Allen ho
Evonn pl

Loretta pl
Grace M pl
Henry T pl
Leo
Alfred
Rundlett, Winnie G (Small
Rid
*Eldreth A pl E Peru
Russ, H H mill op Rid
Lillian A (Hines ho
Russell, Lydia O (York
R Falls
Mary E (m Clark ho

## S

Sanders, R B harness mkr
Dix
Sargent, Paulina W (Linscott
Rid
*Lillian L (m Poor
Brownfield
*Frank L far Stanley
Almira B (m Kennard
*Della A (m Norton ho
Waldoboro
Sargent, Wm far&guide Hale
Mary E (Coffren ho
Willie V far
Ernest W lab
Daniel H lab
Hayden J pl
Nellie M (m Merchant ho
Sawyer, Walter mill op Rid
Lydia (Meunrer ho

| | |
|---|---|
| Ruby | |
| Walter | |
| Seamar, C H    mason's helper | |
|        Rid | |
|    Hattie E (Brown     ho | |
| Shahan, Edward     mill op | |
|    Alma (Glant | |
| Sharland, Peter    lab     Rid | |
|    Lizzie A (Barsley     ho | |
|    Chester A | |
|    Maria E | |
| Shaw, Millie E     mill op | |
| Sherwood, (Solomon | |
|        ex & truckman | |
|    Jennie R (Burnes     ho | |
|    Edith (m Fisher     ho | |
|    *Dora (m Clark  ——Penn | |
|    *Annie (m Dunn     ho | |
|    16 Magee, Cambridge, Mass | |
|    Lottie     ho | |
|    Lena     stu | |
|    *Nettie U (m Fernandus | |
|        Penn | |
| Shortman, Harold L     pl | |
|        Hale | |
| Shortman, Joseph     Hale | |
| Simson, Albert     car | |
|    Maria (Dagle     ho | |
|    Armand | |
|    Blanche | |
| Singer, N S    mill op     Rid | |
|    Victoria M (Eno     ho | |
|    Frank G     mill op | |
|    Agnes M     ho | |

Edward N     mill op
Archie P     stu
Small, Leon M    bk kpr    Rid
Clarice O (Thayer     ho
Clarice A
Small, Lewis E     mill op
Mabel R (Harris     ho
Small, Albert E     car
Helena O (Park     ho
Clifford O     pl
Smart, Everett L    millwright
Mary E (Dearborn     ho
Harold D     pl
Lloyd C     pl
George H
Smith, Owen P    agt & auct'r
Lucy T (Smith     ho
Samuel T     elec
Chester O     mill op
Frank H     stu
Smith, Jesse H    blk     Dix
Lydia H (Kidder     ho
Smith, Louise (Babcock    Dix
Mary F (m Forester
       ho & seamstress
Freeman B     far
*Chas F    far    Rumford
*Albert W    s mill op    Dix
Smith, Ben A    lab     Rid
Mabel F (Kimball     ho
Smith, Wm H    box shp    Rid
*Chas A     mach
     18 Smith, Portland

| | | |
|---|---|---|
| *Clinton C | restaurant | |
| Pride's Cor, Portland | | |
| *Callie L (m Leighton | | |
| W Falmouth | | |
| *Clark S | shop op | Mass |
| Bertha A (Blanchard | | ho |
| Spaulding, Earle W | | car |
| Martha S (Reed | | ho |
| Spaulding, Dan'l | agt | Rid |
| Laura (Abbott | | ho |
| Almira B (m Clement | | ho |
| Myrtie W (m Wills | | ho |
| Stanchfield, G C | bk kpr | Rid |
| Jennie R (Quinn | | ho |
| Wallace C | | |
| Marjorie H | | |
| Stanley, Chas L | | mer |
| Wilmer E (Mason | | ho |
| Steves, Hiram | | teamster |
| Stevens, Edw R | | mer |
| Harriet R (Brett | | ho |
| Thos M | | liveryman |
| Stevens, Chas | | lab |
| Stevens, Thos M | | liv stable |
| Louise C (Gigger | | ho |
| Stevens, Geo A | mer | Rid |
| Mary J (Hayford | | ho |
| *Edith M (m Harlow | | ho |
| Smith's Crossing, R Falls | | |
| Stevens, Wallace C | livery | Rid |
| Carrie (Wills | | ho |
| Stevens, Alice L | mill op | Rid |
| Stora, Jennie M (Richards | | ho |
| Geo B | | guide |

| | | |
|---|---|---|
| Storer, Moses K | | far |
| Sumner, Chas A | lab | Rid |
| Abbie E (Goff | | ho |
| Swett, Sarah J (Moorey | | ho |
| Samuel M | | mill op |
| Geo I | | car |
| Frances M (m Penley | | ho |
| Swett, I H | fireman | Rid |
| Blanche L (Phillips | | ho |
| Stanton L | | |
| Stanwood O | | |
| Lucille L | | |
| Swett, Benj B | clerk | Rid |

## T

| | | |
|---|---|---|
| Targy, Paul | mill op | R Falls |
| Clemina (Blott | | ho |
| Targy, Jos | mill op | R Falls |
| Targy, Fred | lab | R Falls |
| Taylor, J W | prin H S | Rid |
| Ella L (Farmer | | ho |
| Taylor, M A | far | Hale |
| Laura E (Soule | | ho |
| *Myrtie (m Shatney | | ho |
| Clarksville, N H | | |
| Carrie E (m Flagg | | ho |
| *Ella (m Hodgdon | | |
| Roxbury | | |
| Edward W | | lab |
| Flossie E | | stu |
| Pearl S | | stu |
| Charles E | | pl |
| Taylor, R L | far | Frye |

Julia A (Goff                    ho
Wallace F   far & wood dlr
Charles F   far & wood dlr
Mary E                           tr
Randall Leroy                    tr
Frank                            pl
Nathaniel                        pl
Therrier, Jos    lab    R Falls
Amelia (Fornier
Peter                            pl
Emile                            pl
Eva                              pl
Willie
Mabel
Tilley, Dora M (Cole            Rid
Avis                             pl
Eva                              pl
Todd, Jno    boss in mill    Rid
Agnes (Craig                    ho
Jno Jr                           pl
Clarence                         pl
Frank H
Toothaker, I P          fireman
                                Rid
Eva F (Harlow               ho
Toothaker, W U  RR eng  Rid
Jennie F (Royal             ho
Towne, Charlotte M
               (Stockwell   Rid
Mabel T (m Hanley
               Hotel Ridlon
Trask, John R    lawyer   Dix
Trask, Louise        ho   Dix
Trask, Oscar F       far   Dix

Jane E (Edmunds          ho
*Harriet E                   t
840 Franklin ave,Cleveland, C
*Wade C                   bk kp
               Mechanic Falls
Betsey M (m Horn         ho
Albert S                 cler
Trask, Ernest L  p mill op  Ri
Jennie J (McLean         ho
Pearl
Tripp, Sylvia M (Babb      ho
Cora D
Tucker, B V       lab       Ri
Tucker, M E      mach      Di
Frances C (Aiken          h
Fred A                   mac
Marcella F                h
Charles P                  p
Turner, Linwood B        la
Turner, C E   stone mas    Ri
Bessie P                  h
Foster C                   F
Gerald E                   F
Lewis A

### V

Vagg, W J         lab       Ri
Vandenburgh, W E            Ri
               master mec
Esther A (Lamb           h
Arthur R                 mec
Edith A   R Times report
Van Kirk, Jesse W     mill o

|  |  |  |  |
|---|---|---|---|
| Mary A (Shaw | ho | Rose E (m Haines | ho |
| Winnifred A | | Virgin, Albert D | cl |
| Varney, Edw D eng | Rid | Minnie E (Maxwell | ho |
| Rachel M (Curtis | ho | Thelma P | |
| *Bertha M (m Pattee | ho | | |
| No Stratford, N H | | **W** | |
| Leslie O | eng | | |
| Arthur L | mill op | Wagner, Wm | mill op |
| Harold C | pl | Maggie E (—— | ho |
| Varney, L O | eng | Percey, D | stu |
| Carrie S (Reed | ho | Wagner, S B | mill op |
| Hazel M | | Alice M (Smith | ho |
| Louise S | | Valletta M | pl |
| Vaughan, Reuben mill op | Rid | Lillian P | |
| Vinnie M (Maloon | ho | Waite, John H | mill op |
| Inez D | | Eliza M (Williams | ho |
| Vaughan, Dorcas (Greenlaugh | | Waite, R D dentist | Rid |
| | Rid | Laura V (Young | ho |
| *Angus lab | Cal | Eleanor F | |
| *Arthur | far | Wakefield, A W mill op & car | |
| Lunburg Co, N S | | C T (Moore | ho |
| Virgin, Addie L (Brown | ho | Wakefield, H L pattern mkr | |
| Virgin, Flora J (—— | ho | | R Falls |
| *Etta M (m Worthley | | Ida M (Dearborn | ho |
| R Falls | | Marion E | |
| Harry O | stu | Walker, Cynthia M (Dorr | ho |
| Virgin, Wm P far & milkman | | Walker, Betsy E (Miner | ho |
| Mabel B (Taylor | ho | Elvira E (m Knowlton | |
| Stanley F | | Walker, W F car | Hale |
| Stanward W | | Ezma L (Emery | ho |
| Virgin, B F | car | Eltie | lab |
| Ella F (Raymond | ho | Walker, Alex cook | Rid |
| Edwin E | car | Catherine (McDougall | ho |
| Albert R | cl | May A | |

| | | | |
|---|---|---|---|
| Vincent A | | | |
| Wallace, Maggie J | | mill op | |
| Warner, A G | clerg | Rid | |
| Watson, Jos | | steam fit | |
| Nettie (Moffett | | ho | |
| Ervin J | | | |
| Weeks, Thos L | | | |
| Jane C (Glover | | ho | |
| Ernest L | | pl | |
| Lina C | | pl | |
| Nellie C | | pl | |
| Ralph R | | pl | |
| Weeks, S J | far | Hale | |
| Lillian M (Eastman | | ho | |
| Vestie J | | pl | |
| Chas L | | pl | |
| Ola M | | | |
| Weeks, Joshua F | far | Hale | |
| Thomas L | | far | |
| Welch, Geo M | car | Rid | |
| Elizabeth M (Booker | | ho | |
| Joseph B | | pl | |
| Marcia L | | pl | |
| Lura M | | | |
| George E | | | |
| Welch, W L, | car & bld | Rid | |
| Tena M (Burgess | | ho | |
| Dora M | | pl | |
| Wescott, W L | | | |
| chief eng Ox mill | | Rid | |
| Mary B (Lebalister | | ho | |
| Guy R | | stu | |
| Mildred B | | stu | |
| Merle W N | | pl | |

| | | | |
|---|---|---|---|
| White, Henry | far | Dix | |
| White, T F | far | Dix | |
| Augusta (Ford | | ho | |
| White, George | | lab | |
| Josephine (Martin | | ho | |
| Joseph | | | |
| Frank | | | |
| John | | | |
| Josephine M | | | |
| Jennie | | | |
| Lucy | | | |
| White, M C | far | Dix | |
| Harriet C (Brown | | ho | |
| Whitehead, John | | | |
| p mill op | | Rid | |
| Whitman, C E (Hutchins | | Rid | |
| Charles B | | far | |
| Alphonso | | mill op | |
| Whitman, Chas H | far | Rid | |
| Lawrence A | | pl | |
| Annie L | | pl | |
| Margaret L | | pl | |
| Iva M (Hemmenway | | ho | |
| Avis M | | | |
| Whitman, H B | far | Rid | |
| Virgil H | | pl | |
| Florence M | | pl | |
| Addie E | | pl | |
| Elizabeth M (Dorr | | ho | |
| Carl B | | | |
| Whitman, Winnie G (Rundlett | | | |
| | | Rid. | |
| Whitmore, E C | far | Dix | |
| Ida M (Smith | | ho | |

| | | |
|---|---|---|
| *Arthur C | | lab |
| | Atkinson, N H | |
| *Herbert L | mill op | Dix |
| *Harry E | mill op | Dix |
| *Ella M (m Hall | | Dix |
| George M | | mill op |
| Joshua H | | lab |
| *Florence M (m York | | |
| | | Peru |
| Fred A | | lab |
| William H | | pl |
| Gladys B | | pl |
| Edwin C Jr | | pl |
| Ralph G | | pl |
| Frank F | | |
| Whitmore, I P | fire | Rid |
| Ida M (Beal | | ho |
| Beulah A | | pl |
| Ernestine M | | pl |
| Thelma A | | pl |
| Whitney, O E | mill op | Rid |
| A H (Barrett | | ho |
| Whitney, Clara E (Taylor | | Rid |
| Manilla F | | pl |
| Whooley, Geo J | mill op | Rid |
| Mary B (Belas· | | ho |
| Leo G | | pl |
| Elizabeth | | |
| Henry | | |
| William E | | |
| Wiggett, E G | | sawyer |
| Nellie A (Hutson | | ho |
| Edwin G Jr | | pl |
| Willett, John | | mill op |

| | | |
|---|---|---|
| Alphonsine (Caron | | ho |
| Napoleon | | pl |
| Willoughby, A S (Austin | | Dix |
| *Frank L | mill op | Dix |
| Austin | cl | Dix |
| Sadie M | box mkr | Dix |
| Willoughby, E B | butcher | Dix |
| Persie E (Beedy | | ho |
| Wills, Arthur E | eng | Rid |
| Sadie L (Bennett | | ho |
| Florence E | | pl |
| Lillian A | | |
| Wills, Geo R | plumber | Rid |
| Myrtie W (Spaulding | | ho |
| Lucile M | | pl |
| Wing, I S | p mill | Rid |
| Josie M (Wing | | ho |
| Wing, Saml F | lab | Hale |
| Joanna L (Wing | | ho |
| Plinny V | | lab |
| Wing, Mary (Wing | | Hale |
| Winnifred A (m Frost | | |
| *Lillian L (m Johnson | | ho |
| Isaac S | | mill op |
| *Maria T (m Phelps | | ho |
| | | East Rumford |
| *Lois E (m Fish | | |
| | | Boston, Mass |
| Wing, I F | | far & millman |
| Hannah B (Haines | | ho |
| *Esty H | far | East Madrid |
| Elsie M | | pl |
| Milo H | | pl |
| Huldah B | | pl |

Winslow, J C    time kpr    Rid
  Olive A (Littlefield        ho
Withee, Mary O (Goodrich  ho
  John M                   mach
Wood, J F   fore mill   R Falls
  Mary E (Dowling           ho
  James H             mill op
  Matilda J                 stu
  John F Jr                  pl
  Annie E
Wood, Walter M       mill op
  Annie S (Madison          ho
Woodward, D W             Rid
  Julia E (Marden           ho
  *F E   cl   Livermore Falls
  Mildred B (m Hanlon
  Louise M (m Foster
Worthley, Homer   lab   Hale
  Ida M (Bradeen            ho
  Helen E
  Harold A
Worthley, A A     far    Hale
  Ada F (Taylor             ho

*Fred A       Riverside, Cal
      supt elec light plant
*Effie May (m Robbins  ho
                   Frye Sta
*Leon E         millwright
               Berry Mills
*Elmer M           R Falls
  asst supt paper bag mill
Worthley, Selden E    mill op
  Lulu M (Wood            ho
  Seiden B                pl
  Georgia M               pl
  Annie L
Wright, S E             team
  Ethel M (Jordan         ho
Wyman, John W   eng   Rid
  May E (Else             ho
  Walter M

                Y

Young, Milton            car
  Amy E (Wallace          ho

# CENSUS OF PERU

POSTAL DIRECTIONS: When no address is given **PERU** is understood. Other addresses are abbreviated as follows: West Peru, R F D 1—West 1; East Peru—East; West Peru—West; Peru Center—Ctr.

## A

Abbott, A A      far & clerg West 1

Allen, O C      far      West 1
  Anna S (Jose      ho
  William E      lab
  Edith R (m Chenery      ho

Ames, Mary W (Griffin West 1
  *Geo C      ins & mill op Monmouth
  *Mary E (m Lord Monmouth

Andrews, Chas   far   West 1
  Nellie J (Bowker      ho

Andrews, H H.   far   West 1
  Mary E (Wing      ho

Andrews, Ernest  far  West 1
  Etta M (House      ho
  Iva M

Andrews, Blanche J (Woodsum   East
  Ethel E

Arnold, Ida J (Burgess   West

Arnold, J A  miller & grain dlr West

Arnold, W L      miller   West
  Osca M (m Putnam      ho

Atkins, M S      far      West
  Sarah W (Lothrop      ho
  Velma L (m Newton      ho
  *Edith L (m Dickeman Rumford Falls
  *Willie E   far & milkman Dixfield
  Alice M (m Hall

Atkins, A W      car      West
  Aurie E (Hammond      ho
  Ralph E      car
  Clarence E      pl

Austin, B S      far      West
  Etta A (Burgess      ho
  William G

Austin, Erwin   mill op   West
  Gladys M (Knox   mill op

Austin, Aruo J   car   West
  Alice I (Newell      ho
  Leland E      pl

Oscar N pl
Lawrence C
Austin, E G millman West
Emma A (Knights ho
Arno J car
Erwin R mill op
Averill, Sophia A (Reed East
Harland E mill op

**B**

Babb, Dolly K (Peabody
East
*Clinton R far
Livermore Ctr
Elda H (m Luce ho
Babb, Leroy O far East
Bessie M (Purington ho
Gladys M
Marguerite L
Barrett, P G mer
V M (Holman ho
Mona M pl
Celia F
Bassett, E G East
far & cream coll
May (Harlow ho
Fred H pl
Bean, Mary A (Estes West
*Fannie M (m Abbott ho
Rumford Falls
*Sylvanus M far Minot
*Chas W tr
Bearce, B A far & mill West
Informationed withheld

Bent, W H P M
Mary E A (Barrows ho
Berry, Lillian E (Hodsdon
West
Carroll T pl
*Marion pl Andover
Bishop, Hannah B (Lovejoy
*M L watch fact op
Trenton, N J
Bowke, H B far West 1
Boynton, Gardner B far
East
Sarah J (Small ho
*Fannie I (m Fraser ho
Farmington, Mass
*Geo W smkr Lynn, Mass
*Emma F (m Tuell ho
Merrimack, Mass
*Mary E (m Bee ho
Lowell, Mass
*Lillian M (m Kemp ho
Kingston, N H
*Arthur W car blk
Merrimack, Mass
Brackett, Sarah M (Jackson
West
*Leslie mill op Auburn
*Ervin s shop
Brockton, Mass
Brown, Arthur W lab West
Geneva D (Haines ho
Brown, Jane E (Witham West
Elmer E far
Celeste A mill

Marcia L (m Hall     ho

Burgess, Lewis   t p mill   West

    Carrie E (Burgess     ho

    Myrtie B (m Woodbury

    Leon F     team

    Florence S     mill op

    Flora M     pl

    Archer A     pl

Burgess, Sarah C (Zwicke

          West

    Ada J (m Arnold     ho

    Etta A (m Austin     ho

    Ida M ( m Demerit     ho

Burgess, L R    far    West 1

    Minnie A (Nash     ho

    Olive E

    Goldie I

Burgess, John    far    West 1

    Mary J (Robinson     ho

    Clyde C     pl

    Archie J     pl

    O R     pl

Burgess, E T    far    West 1

Burgess, H R    far    West 1

    Emma S (Lovejoy     ho

    Alton L .     far

    Lena M     pl

Burgess, Albert A    car    West

    Ina M (Fish     ho

## C

Campbell, H F    car    West

    Lilla E (Rowe     ho

    Mabel E     pl

    Winnefred V

Capin, Emma J (Burbank     ho

    *Curtis L    mill op    Jay

Card, Emma C (Dixon     ho

    Etta E (m Child     ho

Chase, Angelia (Shackley

          East

    *Chas C    lab    Canton

Chase, Henry A    far    East

    Priscilla C (Kidder     ho

Chase, Hattie M (Shackley

          West

Chenery, D C    lab    West 1

    Edith R (Allen     ho

    Gladys M

    Wilber H

Chenery, D L    far    West 1

    David C     lab

    *Maud L (m Driscoll     ho

       Livermore Falls

Childs, Wm W    far    West 1

    Etta E (Card     ho

    Harold L     pl

    Harland G     pl

    Hayden E

    Helen T

    Geneva M

Childs, C N    far & millman

          West 1

    Nellie D (Lovejoy     ho

    Leon W     pl

Childs, E F    far    West 1

    Hannah J (Wing     ho

*Anna M (m Robbins
          Rumford Falls
*Emily J (m Edwards    ho
          Phillips
*Albert F           mill op
          Livermore Falls
*Jas D              mill op
          Livermore Falls
*Lewis A    far    Phillips
Perley B               lab
Benjamin H             lab
Childs, Perley K    far    East
Helen D (Howard        ho
Harold P               pl
Childs, Arthur B   lab   East
Childs, Viola B (Wing  West 1
Chas N        far & millman
*Geo V                 lab
          No Woodstock
William W              far
Arthur L               lab
*Mary E (m——           ho
     R F D Bryants Pond
Percy E             mill op
Clarence E          mill op
Childs, Elbridge G     far
Anna M (Hammond        ho
Elmer L
Childs, Arthur E Jr    West
Clark, Horace A        East
Alice J (Irish      dr mkr
Charles F
Conant, Danl II    far    Ctr
Annie R (Lewis         ho

Conant, J E   far & cream coll
                       Ctr
Emma J (Shea           ho
George H               far
Daisy M                stu
Coolidge, C E    far   West 1
Julia B (Wing          ho
Coolidge, Arthur G  pl  West
Cote, Mary V (Ames   West 1
*Emma L (m Pingree     ho
                    Canton
Cox, Wm H       far    East
Cox, Emery E    far    East
Edith M (Curtis        ho
Helena A               pl
Beulah E
Cox, Chas H     far    West
Ruth A (Hall           ho
Cummings, Danl C far West 1
Mary A (Bean           ho
Curtis, Alvah M   far  West
Addie E (Hall          ho
Hazel M                pl
Curtis, Eliza H (Frye  East
Curtis, W F     far    East
Harriet A (Butler
Edith M (m Cox         ho
Frank E         s shop op
*Clara E (m Churchill  ho
          Johnsonburg, Pa
Alma E         mill op & cl

# D

Davenport, Leonard H          far
  Elnora B (Knight          ho
  Ernest W          mill op
Davenport, Cyrus          far
             West 1
  Lucy F (Allen          ho
  *Fred H          ptr
     17 South, Auburn
  *Herbert B  far  Skillings
Delano, O R     far     West 1
  Josephine M (Fletcher  ho
Delano, Daniel D          far
  Laura (Burgess          ho
  Rosie L          ho
  Ernest O          lab
Delano, Fannie H (Jackson
  Oscar R          far
  *Hattie M (m Leadbetter
             Auburn
  Lottie D (m Hammond
  Annie M (m Putnam  ho
  Deforest O          far
Demerit, Frank     far     West
  Rosann P (Knight          ho
  Jas L          elec moterman
  Edward S          mill op
  *Chas C          laundry del
            R Falls
  Etta A          mill op
  Abbie M          mill op
Demerit, Edw S          mill op
            West

  Ada M (Burgess          ho
  Ethel M          pl
Demerit, E E     far     West
  V L (Hodsdon          ho
  Ariel I          pl
Deshon, M T     far     East
  *Ellis F          s shop op
            Auburn
  Wallace S          R R ser
Dorr, Eva          ho  West 1
Eastman, Alice F (Burgess
            West
  Lucy M (m Floyd          ho
  Charles R          mill op
  Victor A          lab

# F

Farrer, Thos     far     East
  Prudence W (Bemis          ho
Fletcher, Danl     far     West 1
  Henrietta, D (Buck          ho
  Josephine M (m Delano
Fletcher, Everett B          far
  Cora B (Knight          ho
  *Mary M (m Shea          ho
        Rumford Falls
  Bennie E          pl
Fletcher, Clifton B          team
  Carrie E (Perry          ho
  Grace
Floyd, A H     mill op     West
  Lucy M (Eastman          ho
  Walter L

Arthur L
Arline F
Floyd, H F          mer     West
    Martha A (Hopkins      ho
    *Florence L (m Hunton
                        Milford
    Flora E (m Knight      ho
    Arthur H           mill op
    *Alice M (m Babb   Mexico
    *Mabel L (m Turner
                    No Turner
    Henry L            mill op
Fogg, C D sec fore No 2, West
    Emma A (Reed          ho
    Albert A              lab
Frost, Sylvester   far    West
    Mary (Burgess         ho
    *Elias B mill op  Madison
Frost, Oscar L     far   West 1
    Cora E (Lovejoy       ho
    Perley O           mill op
    Cleveland V        mill op
    Wilmer M              pl
Frost, John     sec hd    West
    Lillian A (Knox       ho
    Erland      .         pl
    Clavis
Fuller, E M        far   West 1
    Nellie (Price
    Mattie B              pl
    Annie M               pl
    Edwin E               pl

## G

Gammon, J M    retd   West 1
    *Oscar M · watch case mkr
                    Brooklyn, N Y
    *Ida M (m Goodnow
                        dr mkr
    620 9th, So Boston, Mass
    *Chas L           theatre
    113 End, So Boston, Mass
Gammon, Otis    watch rpr
    Eva E (m Walker       ho
Gammon, Elroy M          far
    Cora (Turner          ho
    Louise E              stu
    Hollis S              pi
Getchell, J T      lab    East
    Eunice E (Kneeland    ho
    *Daisy (m McKenney
    *Bernice D            lab
                    Lower Maine
    Randall A             lab
    Ernest C              lab
Getchell, S A      far    East
    Hattie M (Stillman    ho
    Albert E              pl
    Stella                pl
    Clyde E
Gillespie, Wm B          far
    Esther L (Babb        ho
    Winnie Belle
Gillespie, Wm      far   West 1
    Elizabeth (McKee      ho

*Andy                       bk kpr
      Gloucester, Mass
Robert                         far
W B                            far
*Mary J (m Merchant   ho
      Lensville, Mass
*Janette (m Herrick      ho
      Gloucester, Mass
*Margaret (m McPhee   ho
      Rumford Falls
*Lizzie (m Welch          ho
      Rumford Falls
Gillespie, Robt               far
M B (Knight                 ho
Goding, Dana W    far    East
  Eltene E (Virgin          ho
  Mabel F                      tr
Goding, G W      mer    West
  Floriell (Bryant
  G Ernest                   mer
  Edward L                    pl
Goggin, John E   far   West 1
  May L (Thurston
  Bertha L                     tr
  *Clarence J      steam fit
      239 Congress, Portland
  Sidney C                     pl
Gorden, G B     far    West 1
  Flora A (Wyman          ho
  Leslie L                      pl
  Jennie H                     pl
  Mary
  George G

Gordon, Wm W  far & butcher
                            West
  Pamelia E (Stevens     ho
  Bertha L                     pl
Gordon, C F      far      West
  Louise (Wing              ho
Gowell, J W        car     West
  Aurilla E (Lovejoy      ho
  Susie G (in Haines      ho
Gowell, Elizabeth M (St Clair
                            West
  *Geo W            s shop op
                      Lynn, Mass
Griffin, Mary (Pettingill
                           West 1
  Mary V (m Hotham
  *Delbert C                 far
                    Roberts, Wis
  *Eliza G      Mattoon, Wis
  *Vilda A (m Howland   ho
                    Dummer, N H
  *Rebecca H (m Hotham
                    Rumford Falls
Guptill, Charles W          far
  Jennie E (Capen          ho
  Marshall C                  pl
  Bertha G
  Nellie E

## H

Hadley, Albert G  far    East
  Vienna A (Cox            ho
  Alice J          ·           pl
  Meriam L                   pl

Chas H       pl
Florence A
Infant
Haines, Edw A     cabinet mkr
      West
   Lillian E (Berry     ho
   Rodney E     pl
   Bertha L     pl
   Alice J
Hall, Noah    far    West
   *Gertrude (m Snell    ho
     So Framingham, Mass
Hall, Alice J    ho    West
Hall, Mandeville    far    Ctr
   Marcia (Varney   ho & tr
   Alfred V     stu
   Marion G     tr
   Alice P     tr
   Mildred    ho & stu
   Ruth     stu
   John L     pl
   Louise     pl
Hall, Josiah    far    West 1
   Geo W    millman & far
   Chas A    millman & far
   Ella A (m Curtis     ho
   Albert H    fore t p mill
   Josiah G    far & millman
Hall, G W    far & millman
      West 1
   Marcia L (——     ho
   Myrtle Z     pl
   Leonard D     pl
Hall, A H fore t p mill West 1

Gertrude E (McEgan    ho
Lawrence G    pl
Lester A
Hamilton, Mrs ——     East
Hamilton, Mary A (Witham
      West
Hammon, Herbert far West 1
Hammond, A C   far & crm col
      West 1
   Lottie B (Delano     ho
   Stanley J     lab
   Lalia M     pl
   Stewart N     pl
Haines, Wallace E    mill op
      West
   Orrie E (Austin     ho
   Clarence E
Harlow, N D    far    East
   Cora A     ho
   *Carroll A    miner & far
      Oregon
   *Clarence G lumb Hanover
   *Sadie J (m Smith
     73 Bates, Lewiston
   Arthur L     far
   *Willard S barber Auburn
   *Lucy F (m Morrill     ho
      Norwich, Conn
   *Ralph L     millman
      Hanover
Hazelton, Lydia J (Hazelton
   Lizzie M (m Walker     ho
Hazelton, Arthur S     far
   Lena M     tr

Dora H    stu
Sidney A    pl
Gertrude H    pl
Holman, A S    far & butcher
   East
Lona W (Hines    ho
*Fred C ptr Cleveland, O
Grace B (m Russell    ho
*Guy F ptr Cleveland, O
Carl S    cl
*Florence M ho Portland
Edith M    pl
Harold L    pl
Hopkins, John    far West 1
Mary E (Looney    ho
*Jennie M (m Wyman    ho
   Rumford Falls
Willie A    far
Hopkins, Mary R (Abbott    ho
Bertha E (m Searles    ho
Hopkins, O C    far West 1
Alice M (Roberts    ho
Merle R    pl
Hosdon, G    lab
*Lula (m Dunn    Byron
*Gertrude (m Young    ho
   W Minot
*Addie (m Young
   Kingfield
*Jarvis mill op Kingfield
Addie (Lane    ho
Hotham, W S    far West 1
Mary V (Ames    ho
Chas C    pl

Howard, S W    far West 1
Emily M (Babb    ho
Helen D (m Child
Estella M    tr
Myrtle A    tr
William H    lab
Malva E    ho
Wallace W    pl
Howard, Chas J    far West 1
Nettie M (Gammon    ho
Howard, E M    mill & far East
Eunice T (Oldham    ho
*Julia F (m French
   Livermore Falls
*Lillian S (m Dyke    ho
   Livermore Falls
Earle    lab
Edna E    stu

Irish, Lorenzo E    far East
Mary H (Kidder    ho
Frank E    pl
Leslie H    pl
Wilbur C
Irish, Betsey J (Godwin    East
Alice J m Clark    ho
Emerson A    far
Ethel T    ho
Irish, Jas E    far East
Vesta E Weeks    ho
*Lovinia D    nurse
   Worcester, Mass

Benj S                          pl
Cephas E                        pl

## J

Jackson, Samuel
        far & fox hunt    East
Johnson, A M        far    East
    Mary (Goodenow          ho
    *Grace L (m Hutchins    ho
                Mechanic Falls
    *Fred   barber   Lewiston
    Edith M                 ho
    William I              far
    *Lillian (m Hatch  Carmel
    Guy E                   pl
Jordan, Addie M (Lunt   West
    William L               pl
    Maurice A               pl

## K

Keene, Lydia C (Abbott
                    West 1
    *Ora E (m Leonard       ho
                    Mansfield
Kidder, Sarah M (Brackett
                    West
Kidder, C H            far
    Matilda J (White       ho
    *Cora M (m Litchfield  ho
    19 Mineral, Redding, Mass
    Ervin C              mer
    Lena C
    Wilma B        tr & mer

    Ethel B             mill op
Kidder, E C                mer
    Hattie B (Holman        ho
    Ethlyn M
    Kenneth I
Kidder, B C        far     East
    Sadie E (Castle
    · Elwood C              pl
    Hazel G
    Sibyl M
Kimball, Frank   far   West 1
Knight, O L     far    West 1
    C Louise (Brown         ho
    J L                     pl
    Ralph G
    Blanche E
Knight, Mary G (Shaw West 1
Knight, F A     team    West
    Flora E (Floyd          ho
Knight, Mabel              Ctr
Knight, Lora M dr mkr  East
Knight, Adna W    far    Ctr
    Ada E (Gerrish          ho
Knight, Danl W    far    Ctr
    Lydia J (Burgess        ho
    *Leroy W               mer
        96 Wash, Auburn, N Y
    ·Cora B (m Fletcher     ho
Knox, D D     far     West 1
    B (Roberts             ho
    Elmer W                far
    *Chester L     car     Rid
    Angie A                ho
    *Frank L mill op  Dixfield

| | | | |
|---|---|---|---|
| Knox, Sumner N | far | West | |
| Mary E (Martin | | ho | |
| *Sarah E (m Leadbetter | | | |
| s op | Lynn, Mass | | |
| Gladys M (m Austin | mill op | | |
| Knox, Melvin | far | West | |
| Knox, Lona L (Knight | | | |
| | | West 1 | |
| Linwood P | | mill op | |
| Edith May | | mill op | |
| Knox, Elmer W | far | West 1 | |
| Flora C (m McIntire | | ho | |
| Elmer L | | far | |
| Lona L (Knox | | ho | |
| Selma M | | ho | |
| Laura B | | ho | |
| Chester L | | pl | |
| Iva M | | pl | |
| Mabel A | | pl | |
| Herbert E | | pl | |
| Elmer W Jr | | pl | |
| Margaret L | | | |
| Knox, Lizzie T (Knight | | | |
| | | West 1 | |
| Ernestine M (m Stillman | | | |
| Ethel A (m Knox | | ho | |
| *Grace M | table girl | | |
| | Paris Hill | | |
| Elwin C | | pl | |
| Gerald E | | pl | |
| Harold A | | pl | |
| Knox, Evanda B | far | West 1 | |
| Lizzie T (Knox | | ho | |
| Merle B | | pl | |

| | | | |
|---|---|---|---|
| Sadie L | | | pl |
| Adeline G | | | |
| Knox, Harry S | far | West 1 | |
| Knox, Elmer L | far | West 1 | |
| Ethel A (Knox | | ho | |
| Knox, J R | far | West 1 | |
| Sarah M (York | | ho | |
| Chandler B | | far | |
| Evanda B | | far | |
| Charles W | | far | |
| Walter E | | far | |
| Knox, Perley G | far | West | |
| Perley L | | mill op | |
| Edith M | | mill op | |
| Leann M (Morrison | | ho | |
| Eula A | | pl | |
| Addie M | | pl | |
| Burchard B | | pl | |
| Vivian D | | | |
| Knox, Chas E | far | West | |

## L

| | | | |
|---|---|---|---|
| Laughton, Thos | lab | East | |
| Leavitt, John | far | West | |
| Isabel F (Burgess | | ho | |
| Malinda A (m Burgess | | ho | |
| Libby, Lark | retd | East | |
| Libby, Geo H | far | East | |
| Rosanna E (Poland | | ho | |
| *Herbert R | | far | |
| Box 204, Abbington, Mass | | | |
| Rose C | | ho | |
| Linus A | | | |

Lovejoy, Celia D (Bishop　ho
　Elmer L　　　　supt R R
Lovejoy, Jos H　far　　West
Lovejoy, Lucius K far West 1
　Addie E (Morrill　　　ho
　Alton L　　　　　　　pl
Lovejoy, Benj　　　　West
　Ada B (Peavy　　　　ho
Luce, Chas S　　mer　East
　Elda H (Babb　　　　ho
　Fred
　J Merton
*Ludden, John N　　　　far
　　　　　　Malden, Mass
　Josephine S (Carver　East
　*Herbert S　elec　Bath
　Porter　　　　　　far
　Helen J (m Oldham　　ho
Lunt, Herbert H　　　far
　Naoma V (Taylor
　Leo W　　　　　　　pl
Lunt, Celia B (Adkins　West 1
　Addie M (m Jordan　　ho
　*Cora E (m Crockett　ho
　　　　　　　　Dixfield
Lunt, U G　　, far　West 1
　Lizzie L (Soper　　　ho
Lufkin, Nelson　far　West 1

M

Mathews, Chas W　far West 1
Mathews, Cordelia (Weaver
　　　　　　　　West 1

McGraw, Della (Poland　East
　Zephyr M　　　　　pl
McIntyre, U G　far　West 1
　Nellie M (Putnam　　ho
　Leon E　　　　　　pl
　Blanch　　　　　　pl
　Hazel M　　　　　pl
　Harold　　　　　　pl
　Ralph
　Henry S
McIntyre, A B　far　West 1
　Flora E (Knox　　　ho
　Charlotte B　　　　pl
　Mary E　　　　　　pl
　Bernice M　　　　　pl
　Verna E　　　　　pl
　Betsey E
McPherson, Jno J　far　East
　Duncan J　　　　　pl
　Edwin　　　　　　pl
　Daniel L
Miller, Jas W　far　West 1
　Olive V (Norton　　ho
　Mabel L　　　　　　ho
　Pearl L　　　　　　ho
　Glenroy M　　　　　pl
　Evelyn C
Morrill, M G　far & butcher
　　　　　　　　West 1
　Elnora (Jackson　　ho
　*Ernest L　　　　Saco
　　　overseer cotton mill
　*Manley G Killingly, Conn
　　　overseer cotton mill

*Fred G   Norwich, Conn
    overseer cotton mill
  Addie (m Lovejoy    ho
  Lauriston R far & butcher
Morrill, Sylviro (Rowe West 1
  Simeon          far
  Abbie K (m Irish    ho
  J R            far
  Jennie R        tr
Morrill, J R   far    West 1
  Etta A (Wyman     ho
  Jas C         far
Morrill, Simeon   far   West 1
  *Chas W  ex mes  Bangor
  Noami A (Cone      ho

## O

Oldham, Elias S   far    East
Oldham, Merritt H  far   East
  *Clarence H     steam fit
          Granite, Rid
  *Frank D   Rumford Falls
      paper bag mill op
  Willie A          pl
  Harry M.         pl
  Della (McGraw     ho
  Maurice B        pl
Oldham, Emerson   far   East
  Maud L (York      ho
  Leroy F         pl
  Edward E
  Carroll A
Oldham, Geo W    far    East

  Blanch J (Andrews    ho
Oldham, Columbus  far   East
  Eunice T (m Howard   ho
  *Delia R (m Staples    ho
           Canton Pt
  *Leona S (m Beane    ho
       Livermore Falls
  Lovell F         far
Oldham, Lovell F   far   East
  Helen J (Stowell     ho
Oldham, Jno C   far    East
  Emerson E       far
  *Marinda (m Oliver   ho
             Canton
Oldham, Peleg   far    East
  Mary J (Starbird     ho
  *Clista (m Reed    Bemis
Oldham, Jno   far    East
  Sophia A (Averill    ho
  John R
Oldham, D W   far   West 1
  Mary R (Hopkins    ho

## P

Packard, Benj D far   Canton
  Alberta A (Davis     ho
  *Ethel M (m Hussey
             Canton
  Mildred F        pl
  Harold B         pl
Phelps, O M   far   West 1
  Mary D (Cummings   ho
Phinney, W H   far   West 1

Ethel L (Hall                      ho
Pinkham, R A                West 1
            ptr & paper hgr
   *Tressa      s op      Auburn
   Georgia A                     pl
   Philip M                       pl
   Helen I                        pl
   Leon R                         pl
   Leroy
Piper, Dan'l W    far    West 1
   Adaliza M (Fogg            ho
   Elsworth E                  car
Piper, E E       car       West
   Mary E (Glover            ho
Poland, Clinton        far & car
                            East
   Rose G (m Bean           ho
   Wendall C            sta agt
   Delia (O'Neil            ho
   Nellie B                    pl
   Annie M                     pl
Poland, Eunice A (French
                            East
   Clinton           car & far
   *Andrew            plumber
          , Concord, Mass
Putnam, C L      lab     West 1
Putnam, Jos A    far     West 1
   Annie M (Delano         ho
   Cecil I                     pl
   Ceylon E                   pl
   Ronello B                  pl
   Hattie M                   pl
Putnam, J A   mer & mill  West

Malissa G (Burgess         ho
Nellie M (m McTire
Augusta B (m Williams  ho
   *James L                  car
          Stewartsville, N J
Edna E (m Tracy   mill op
Osca M (m Arnold         ho
Oscus                      lab
Annie L                     cl
John A Jr                   pl
Putnam, Ida (Bisbee  West 1
   Bernard C               lab
   E Everett                far
   C L                       far
   Lela G                    stu
   Ralph O                   pl

                R

Richardson Wm O       mill op
                          West
   Estelle M (Stowe       ho
   Vernon W
Richardson, Almeda A
                   (Churchill
   Florence S             ho
   *Alfred E           W Paris
   Herbert R              pl
   Mabel A                pl
Robinson, S F       P M & J P
                          West
   Ella C (Dorr           ho
   *Grace E (m Holt  Dixfield
   Charles M              stu

Robinson, H R    far & barber | Velma M                        pl
May F (Keene             ho | Soper, Lizzie L (Graves   West
Clarence H              far | Cora S                        pl
Ethel L                 stu | Stillman, Emma (Turner    ho
Carroll L                pl | Stillman, Thomas W          far
Robinson, Sabra W (Bisbee | Ernestine M (Knox        ho
Rolls, Thos J     far    East | Gerald T
Edna O (Stillman        ho | Stillman, H E   far & meat dlr
Rowe, Henry   retd   West | West 1
Henry O                 far | Olive M (Conant           ho
Rowe, Geo L    lab   West | Hattie M (m Getchell    ho
Ardella E (Demerit      ho | Olive E (m Rose
Rowe, H O    far    West 1 | Swasey, Benj A     Dent West
Etta L (Carter          ho | Florice E (Hammond    ho
Charles H               lab | Lyman K                     pl
Mary E                  stu |
Marion G                stu | **T**
Russell, John S    far   East | Tracy, Chas J    far   West 1
Grace B (Holman         ho | Melissa J (Farnham      ho
Dana W                   pl | Nellie L                     tr
Fred A                      | Tracy, Osborn O   far  West 1
Julia H (Robinson       ho
Grace M                   pl
**S** | Tracy, R L      far & milk car
Small, Christopher M     ptr | West 1
.                       West | Alma B (Hammond      ho
Betsey F (Durgin        ho | Mildred A                   pl
*Winnie G (m Whitman | Maurice R                  pl
Ridlonville | Gerald                      pl
*Lewis E   mill op  Mexico | Trask, Mary J (Burnham  ho
*Leon M    time kpr   Rid | *Thos H                   Leeds
Smith, Geo S    far   West 1 | *Trask, Saml A    far    Avon
May N (Jewett          ho | Leroy                       pl
Archie E                stu | Delia

Trask, Amanda M (Fox  East
Trask, Chas P      far      East
Trask, Bert L      far      East
Turner, Howard          millman
   Alice M (Jackson          ho
   Nina L                         stu
   Edw H                          pl
Turner, Hollis            far
   Cora T (m Hammond    ho
   Sarah E (Robinson
Turner, Emma (Barber      ho
   Howard              millman

## V

Varney, Albert      lab      Ctr

## W

Walden, Gunner    far    West 1
   Karin (——                   ho
   Eva I                          pl
   Bror J E
Walker, Alfred B far & Ins Ctr
   Mary L (Colby              ho
Walker, Daniel W sta agt Ctr
   Eva E (Gammon            ho
   Mildred E                     pl
   Colby G                       pl
   O Merton                      pl
   Stella M                      pl
   Luena F                       pl
   Wilma E
Walker, C S          far & gard
   Lizzie M (Hazelton       ho

   Iola A                     mus tr
   Alma C                        tr
Walker, W H                   far
   Sabrina (Robinson        ho
Weeks, Vestie E (Soule    East
   *Henry F  sta agt  Bemis
   *Fred A        civil ser stu
         Howard, R I
   *Lizzie M (m Luxton     ho
      Kempt, Queens Co., N S
Whittier, Jennie M (Burgess
             West
   Clara A (m Burgess      ho
   Christina H                 ho
   Cyrus W                    mach
Wiken, Kristine (Joranson
            West 1
   *Brita (m Rehn            ho
        Rumford Falls
   Esbjorn                      far
   John W                        far
Williams, H K      ptr & p hgr
           West 1
   Eustine B (Putnam        ho
   Althie                        pl
Wilson, S A  car & wood turn
            West
   Elizabeth M   Gowell ho
   Chas A             far & car
*Wing, Columbus H          far
      West Farmington
   Sarah F (Lloyd            ho
   Louisa P (m Goding
   Hannah J (m Childs

*Lucy A (m Burnham
      Leeds
*William J far Leeds
*Edgar D far Farmington
*Mary O (m Childs
     So Paris
Wing, I B far  West 1
 Mary J (Trask  ho
Wing, I B Jr  far West 1
 Josie E (Wing  ho
 Clarence A   pl
 Elmer A   pl
Woodbury, O T far & rd com
      West
 Myrtie B (Burgess' ho
 Elizabeth M   pl
Woodsum, N B bk kpr West
 Bertha P (Wyman ho
 Gerald B   pl
 Esther   pl
Worthley, Roscoe K retd
     West

 Lydia H (Hayes  ho
Wyman, Benj D far West 1
 Betsy R (Hall  ho
 Bertha P (m Woodsom
 *Elbridge H  lab
   Rumford Falls
Wyman, John C millman
     West 1
 Abbie F (Robinson ho
 Thomas A  mill op
 Flora A (m Gordon ho
 Florence   ho

## Y

York, Jas P far West 1
 Maud L (m Oldham ho
York, Alton L  far
 Florence M (Whitemore
 Ellery O

# HARTFORD CENSUS

NOTE: The following abbreviations of Post Offices are used in the Census of Hartford: East Sumner—E Sum; East Sumner R F D No. 1—E Sum 1; Canton—Can; Canton R F D No. 1—Can 1; North Turner—No Tur; Brettuns—Bret; Buckfield—B'kfld; Buckfield R F D 2—B'kfld 2.

### A

Abbott, A A     lab    E Sum
  *Susan J (m Warren
               Auburn
  A A Jr
Aley, A H     far     E Sum 1
  Sadie G (m Libby
  Clarence S         far
  Mary P           ho
Allen, W H        Buckfield
    far & car, 2d selectman
  Nancy A (Hutchinson   ho
  Nellie A (m ———      ho
  *Wm H     car     R Falls
  *Frank W   far , Buckfield
  Harry C               pl

  Marhon (m Howard
  Mary
Ames, Guy B     eng     Bret
Andrews, Eben L  .        far
  Lizzie (Bryant
Arsenault, Mary    ho   Bret
Austin, Leonard far     Can 1
  *Willis W   s s op   Auburn
  *Minnie L (m Tripp    Tur
  *Carroll   far Chases Mills
  *Mabel (m Roberts   Bkfld
  Nellie M (Smith        ho
  George P           far
  *Stella M (m Dean So Paris
  Arthur S          lab
  Forest W           pl
Austin C A     far     B'kfld

*Lottie E (m Hawkins
    Ctr Harbor, N H
*Frank E cl Holiness, N H
Olive V                          ho
Barker, P C      far      Can 1
Lucy A (Sampson         ho
Mary E                     ho
Albert C                   pl
Leon S                     pl
Barker, Daniel L   far   Can 1
Idella M (Suckles        ho
Dennis L
Barker, O     far        Can 1
Hannah B (Ludden       ho
Preston C                 far
Barrill, Ida A    ho   B'kfld
Barrill, A T     far    B'kfld
*Wm A            wire mkr
    Worcester, Mass
*Edmond P        wire mkr
    Worcester, Mass
Amos T Jr                 lab
Barrows, O R    far    E Sum
Lucy F (Crooker          ho
Barrows, Roselinda (Robinson
    ·               E Sum
*Geo E      far       Sum
*Maria B (m Goss      Sum
*Julia R (m Jennings  Sum
Bartlett, O    far    E Sum 1
Dorcas (Russell          ho
Horace B                  far
Bartlett, Percy L        far
Bartlett, Cecil O        far

Benson, A B      far      Can 1
*Clarence T Bourne, Mass
*John M                 s op
    No Abbington, Mass
*Benj Y                   car
    Whitman, Mass
*Arthur E                 car
    Whitman, Mass
*Stanley M jobber B'l fld
*Sophia H (m Philoon
    Livermore
Benson, C B    far   E Sum 1
Jennie L (Maxim         ho
Arthur W                  far
Ida M                     ho
Frances D                 ho
*Isabel     pl    Hebron
Henry C                   pl
Harry M                   pl
Roland C                  pl
Ethel
Merton
Infant
Berry, Chas H    far    Sum
Sarah E (Hammond      ho
Eunice M                  pl
Berry, Hermon B far  No Tur
Julia H (Turner
Raymond
Jennie F
Adoniron
Berry, Chas H    far    Ctr
Abby F (Robinson       ho
Hermon R                 far

| | | | |
|---|---|---|---|
| Leroy A | car | *Lottie M ('m Grant Leeds | |
| Leon M | far | Ernest E | lab |
| Chas H Jr | pl | Clara I | tr |
| Etta R | pl | Emma E | stu |
| Harlon | pl | Frank A | pl |
| Bicknell, Henry A  far  B'kfld | | Harry T | pl |
| Abby M (Mason | ho | Raymond W | pl |
| Agnes M | ho | Alice | |
| Bicknell, Wm E  far  B'kfld | | Bridgham, F J  far  Bret | |
| Rebecca J (Richmond | ho | Pearl | |
| Edward | law | Amanda M (Flagg | ho |
| *W H W | artist | Briggs, A B  far  Can 1 | |
| Winchester, Mass | | M Emma (Bisbee | ho |
| Billings, Jas H  far  E Sum 1 | | A Montwel | |
| Eva E (Farrer | ho | F Wilber | far |
| James H Jr | pl | Carl B | far |
| Bisbee, Emeline L (Spaulding | | Horace B | stu |
| Can 1 | | Brown, H G  far  Can 1 | |
| Bisbee, Wm C  far  Can 1 | | *Della V (m Peaks | |
| Mabel B (Damon | ho | Santa Cruz, Cal | |
| Francis B | pl | *Effie V (m Taylor | |
| Claud L | pl | Brown, Geo W  far  Ctr | |
| Bonney, Nellie M (Hewett | | Edwin F | far |
| Can 1 | | Emma F (Barker | ho |
| Crystal C | ho | Eda E | pl |
| Bosworth, P  far  No Tur | | Norman G | |
| Maggie (Parnell | ho | Bryant, Edmon  far & blk | |
| Asa C | lab | Can 1 | |
| Lena A | ho | Ruth E (Allen | ho |
| Bosworth, A R  far  No Tur | | Bryant, Edw F  far  Can 1 | |
| Flora A (Prescott | ho | Lovey E (Merrill | ho |
| Otis D | pl | Chas T | lab & pl |
| Bragg, E L  far  Can 1 | | Harold A | pl |
| Annie J (West | ho | Lora M | pl |

Ruby E pl
Jesse G pl
Edmon L pl
Ezra E pl
Ruth G pl
Ida O
Bryant, Fred W    far    Bret
Lilla A (Weston    ho
J Warren    pl
Iva M
Bryant, S E    lab    B'kfld 2
Bryant, Abbie D (Morse
    B'kfld 2
    *Abbie (m Young    No Tur
Burgess, N B    far    E Sum 1
    *Clara O    pl
    277 Minot Ave., Auburn

**C**

Canwell, Chas F    far    Ctr
    Helen B (Robbins    ho
    Addie F    s s op
    Myron R    lab
    Lena M    pl
    Arthur, M (adopted)
Canwell, James M    far    Can 1
    Susie E (French    ho
    Edna M
    Marion I
Carter, Amasa    far    Can 1
    Minnie (Farrar    ho
    Nellie (m Conant    ho
    Rena    ho

Carver, Mary E (Rich    E Sum 1
    *Herbert A    guide
    Andover
Cary, Bethuel    car    E Sum
    Luella F (Foye    ho
Chaln, Frank    far    Canton
    Dalmen (Dorbalbe    ho
    *Melvina (m Fornier
    Oquossoc
    Frank    invalid
    Mary L (m Richards    ho
Chamberlain, Edw    team    Can
    Delia
    Wilfred
    John
Chamberlain, David    far    Can
    *Almira (m Whaling
    New York
    *Louisa (m Dolan    N H
    David    lab
    *Julia (m Landers
    Gardiner
    *Josie (m Lines    New York
    *Joseph    lab    Mass
    Edward    team
    *Louis
    *Fred    lab    N H
    *Ellery    Chester, Md
    *Isreal    lab    N H
    Arthur    lab
    Florence    ho
    Sarah (Gentle    ho
Child, Joseph F    far    E Sum 1
    Mary D (Whitmore    ho

Roscoe J                printer
*Persis A (m Dearborn
                        Canton
Lewis W                 stu
Joseph E                stu
Cloudman, Charlotte L (Lord
                        E Sum 1
   Dorothy A            tr
   Philip H             cl
   Bertrand E           lab
   Avis E               pl
   Robert B L           pl
Colby, Walter M    lab    Bret
   Jennie E (Morse      ho
Cotton, Rufus H  lab  B'kfld 2
Conant, Nellie (Carter   Can 1
   Mildred             pl
   Leon                pl
   Howard              pl
Corbett, Mary C (Reed    ho
   *Emma A     ho    W Peru
Corliss, Geo E          Can 1
   far, blk & 3d selectman
Corliss, David A    far    Ctr
   *Walter        phy & surg
              Yarmouthville
   Alfred C             far
   Lydia J (Stetson     ho
Cox, Alonzo             far
Crockett, Hattie L (Ellis
                        Can 1
   Clementine L         pl
   Reba E               pl
Crockett, Wm T  far  E Sum 1

   Augusta S (Thomas    ho
   Mary E               tr
Cummings, R A  far & cobbler
                        No Tur
   *Lizzie A (m Richardson
                        Winthrop
   *Frank P mill op Hartland
   *Fred E          elec cond
      E Dedham, Mass

# D

Damon, Wilson M         lab
                        B'kfld 2
Davenport, J F    far    Can
   Effie R (Thorn       ho
   Percey A             far
   Wilmer F             pl
Davis, V H     far    E Sum 1
   Rosie V (Poland      ho
   Bernice M
   Valmore V
Davis, Frank K          far
   Rena (Gurney         ho
Dearborn, J H    far    B'kfld
   *Sarah H (m Berry  B'kfld
DeCoster, J B    far   Tur Ctr
   Mattie W (Thurlow    ho
   Mildred E            pl
   Lawrence B
DeCoster, H L          No Tur
   Helen M (Sturtevant
   Harold L             pl
   Austin J             pl

DeCoster, Lester A  far  B'kfld 2
  Lillian M (Berry       ho
  Pearl C              pl
  Donald A           pl
DeCoster, W W     far & car
                 No Tur
Demaris, H   lab   Can 1
  Hosie (Jordan     ho
  Kenneth
Dillingham, Ernest L  far  Ctr
  Lottie E (Small    ho
Dillingham, Jno W    far
  Neda A (Newton    ho
  Elzada G         ho
Dumm, J W  far  B'kfld 2
  Anna R (Grover    ho
  *Geo G  cl  W Harpswell
  *Willard  cl  Harpswell
  Ralph      team & far
  Thos B        car
  Archie E        pl
Dyer, Julian R  far  Sum
  Mabel M (Bisbee   ho
  Raymond B
  Linnie May

### F

Farnum, Jno W  far  Can
  *Maxcellana (m Merrical
            Ft Dodge, Ia
  *Jno F   far  Sumner
  Isaac C        far
  Maude E       ho

  Fred E         far
Farrar, Walter W  far  Can 1
  Lucy B (Tylor     ho
Fletcher, C C   far    Ctr
  Annie T (m Allen
  Florence F (Bonney  ho
  Ethel M         pl
Fletcher, D A  far & agt mach
                Can 1
  Costella D (Ellis    ho
  *D V  lab  Gorham, N H
  *Laura B (m Bryant
    146 Presussic, Portland
  Berdena B (m Ryerson ho
  Cleon E         pl
Fogg, J G   far    Can 1
  Carrie M (Brooks   ho
  *Frank L       car
         Harrison, Mo
  *Cora B (m Barrett
            Portland
  Lillian M (m Paine  ho
  James C         pl
Ford, Eliza A (Bosworth  ho
  *Frank W     barber
        So Portland
  Ida M         ho
Foster, Daniel F  retd  E Sum 1
Foster, F E   far   E Sum
  Sophia H (Robinson  ho
  Stella M        pl
Foster, Eunice S (Shaw  E Sum
Foye, F E  blk   E Sum
  Cora E (Gammon   ho

Francis, C Maria (Beals Can 1
   Rosa M          ho
Fuller, Alonzo  far   No Tur
Fuller, Lydia J (Records
              No Tur
Fuller, A S  far   Livermore
   Mary L (Cates     ho

### G

Gammon, Harold pl E Sum 1
Gammon, Lydia B   B'kfld 2
Gammon, P C  far  B'kfld 2
   Nellie A (Thurlow    ho
   Carl P
Gammon, Hiram II far B'kfld
   Frank          far
   *Flora (m Morrill Auburn
Gentle, Sarah (Shehan   Ctr
   Sadie          pl
*Gilman, J W C      pub co
   76 Sumner, Boston, Mass
   H P (Phinney  ho  B'kfld
   Helen P       office
        Poland Spring
   Bessie H
   Harriet J      actress
   Edmond P        far
   *Wm L stu Providence, R I
   Alice S         stu
Gleason, II M (Bunker  Bret
   *Ada F        s s op
       54 High, Auburn
Glover, Cynthia E (Crockett
           E Sum 1

   Bertie H (m Turner   ho
Glover, B F far & tr E Sum 1
   Ida C (Alley       ho
   Edith E (m Samson   ho
   Ernest C        far
Gorden, Geo  far   Can 1
Gurney, Stilman F   Can 1
   Dexter C       far
Gurney, Chas M  far  Can 1
   Blanch M (Farrington  ho
   Ella M         pl
   Linnie E
   Adney         pl
   Lillian D
Gurney, Rena (Jordan   ho
   Chas         far
Gurney, Dexter C    far
   Fred         pl
   Emery        pl
   Georgia M (DeCoster  ho
   Dexter Jr      pl
   Alice E        pl
   Lester F       pl

### H

Hammond, Sarah E
     (Thompson  ho  Sum
   *Thomas W  far  Sum
   *Henry A   lab  Wilton
   *Chas L  lab    Sum
   *Wesley M  lab   Sum
   *Merton G  far   Sum
   Anna E (m Wing   Sum

Hayford, Wm P      far
   Lewis S      millman
   William L      far
   Glenis E      ho
   Addie M (Marston    ho
Henry, J Fred    far    Can
   Lizzie (Clinch      ho
   Chas F      far
   Lucy E      ho
   Robert W      pl
   Alice M      pl
   Walter E      pl
   Ruth E      pl
   Howard O
   Philamelia E
Hewett, Asa    far    Can 1
   *Clarence E far   Paris, Mo
   *Arthur A      far & car
         Stricklands
   *Cora J (m Roberts   Can
   Nellie M (m Bonney    ho
   *Alfred A      restan
130 Dartmouth, Boston, Mass
   *Dana N (Logan     Kan
Holmes, Geo A     B'kfld 2
   Flora E (Irish      ho
   Bran E      pl
   Earl M      pl
   Lillian F
Howard, H Scott   far   Can 1
   Marhon L (Alley     ho
   *Merton W      op
   11 Waverly, Brockton, Mass

   *Bessie M (m Luce   ho&tr
         Canaan, N Y
Howard, Edwin    far   B'kfld
   *Abbie P (m Willis    ho
         Waltham, Mass
   *Nettie F      watch op
         Waltham, Mass
   *Emily L (m Eames
         Hopkinton, Mass
   *Elisha B      coachman
         Boston
   Abner D      far
Howard, Edith H      pl
Hutchinson, Chas E can & far
   *Hutchinson   pl   Auburn
Huzzey, H O    far   Canton
Hyer, Wm H    lab   B'kfld 2

## I

Irish, Decatur    far   B'kfld 2
   Mary A (Shaw      ho
Irish, Jas E    far   B'kfld 2
   Wilmer M (Maxim    ho
   Howard M      pl
Irish, Edgar E    lumberman
   Lena M (Robbins     ho
   Shirley H      pl
Irish, Orlando      mer
   Lizzie H (Forbes     ho
   Edgar      lumberman
Irish, L O      sta agt
   Elizabeth S
Irish, James      far
   Laura F (——)      ho

## J

Jacobs, H B    far & cream col
                          Can
  Hattie A (Williams        ho
  *Ethel F. (m Farnum
                     E Sumner
  Arthur W                  far
  Alton H                   far
Jones, Mercey L (——
                   Livermore
  Carroll L                 lab
Jones, Lina (Allen       Can 1
  Leonard A                 far
  *Minnie E (m Briggs
                    E Auburn
  Mary L (m Fuller          ho
  *Clara (m Tobin
                   Turner Ctr
  *Nellie B (m Campbell
                      Turner
Jordan, Wm F    far       Ctr
  Olive A (Bryant          ho
  *Rufus O    far      B'kfld
  Lucy F (m Records        ho
  Arthur W                 far
Julius, Jno'H Jr       No Tur

## K

Keene, Mary M (Puffer  Can 1
  M Nettie (m Stetson      ho
  *Fred W          car & bldr
                     Auburn

*Jennie H (m Bonney
                    Sumner
Keene, Ella E    ho      Can 1
Keene, Ezra    far     B'kfld
  Addie F (Robinson        ho
  Harold B                 pl
  Arthur R                 pl
Keene, Lorin A  far  E Sum 1
  Florence M (Turner       ho
  Mildred E                stu

## L

Leavitt, Geo    far   E Sum 1
  Della J (Greenlief       ho
  *Florence E (m Holbrook
                      Stark
Leavitt, Virgil E    far   Bret
  Gladys E                 pl
Lemauex, E    lab        Can
  Celina (Boudier          ho
  Lora                     pl
  Mary L
Lemaux, Felix    far     Can
  Mary (Bushey             ho
  Joseph                   pl
  Josephine                pl
  Henry                    pl
  Fred                     pl
  Edward                   pl
  Rossie
  Wilfred
Leseosseur, E    lab   B'kfld
  Lena (Blonder            ho

Libby, Jas W      B'kfld 2
    far, car & 1st selectman
    *Ida (m Shepherd     ho
             Denver, Col
    Rosa V (Burnham     ho
    Edwin W     far
    *Bessie (m Lucas     B'kfld
    Wm L     far
    Eunice R     tr
Libby, Wm R    far    B'kfld 2
    Sadie G (Alley     ho
    Evelyn A
Lucas, L C    far     Can 1
    Sinora B I (Collis     ho
    Rose M (m Sargent     ho
    Florence E     ho
    *Estelle M (m Bartlett
             Gilbertville
Lucas, Adrian S    far    Can 1

### M

Marston, Jno C    far    Can 1
    Myra A (m Kilbreth
             Livermore
    *Edith E     stu
             Rumford Falls
    Martha A (Sampson
Marston, Abram G   far   Can 1
    Estella S (Kilbreth     ho
    Iva M     pl
    Wilder E     pl
    Earle H     pl
    Allen R

Maxim, Harriet B (Bisbee
             B'kfld 2
    Wilmer M (m Irish     ho
McEachein, D E    paper mkr
             Ctr
    Sarah G (McIntire     ho
    Ernest M
McEachein, Ernest
McPherson, A B   far   E Sum 1
    Christa A (McPherson   ho
    Agnes E     pl
    Martha E     pl
    Minnie Pearl     pl
    Sadie C     pl
    John H
McIntire, H E        R R ser
    Eluora (Parkerson
    Sarah G (m McEachein ho
    Lenora     pl
    Ward S     pl
Mendall, Elvira (Foye   Can 1
    Caleb E     far
Mendall, Caleb E     Can 1
    Clara S (Tyler     ho
Merrill, Elizabeth A
        (Noyes    No Tur
    *Mahala A (m Dunn    ho
           Spring, Auburn
    *Amanda J (m Bosworth
           Hingham, Mass
    *Mary E (m Polley
           Fairhaven, Vt
    C A     far    No Tur
Merrill, C A   far & car   No Tur

Lottie H (Collins  ho
Lovey E (m Bryant
*Lora C    cont & bldr
No Cent ave, Wallaston, Mass
*Lyda H (m Waterhouse
Fayette, Wallaston, Mass
Albert N    con & bldr.
Merrill, A N  car  No Tur
Ida M (Kelliher  ho
Evelyn M  pl
Osman N
Minnick, Caroline A
    (Parkerson
Mitchell, Eliza (Bard  Can 1
*Wallace s s op  Auburn
*Louis H  Bdg ho
    Weymouth, Mass
Abbie A (m Parsons  ho
Mitchell, Wm F  far  Can 1
Lyda J (Mendall  ho
Leora A (m Berry  ho
Wm F Jr  far
Mary A  tr
Mitchell, Clarence I  far Can 1
Grace E C (Thompson  ho
Jno E .  pl
Thelma E
Mank, Levi T  far  B'kfld 2
Stella A (Ames  ho
*Bessie M (m Atkinson
    B'kfld
Moore, A A  far  No Tur
Grace C (Cummings  ho
Russell E

Morse, Lydia R (Putnam  ho
Newton, Addison E  lab
Hattie L (Thompson  ho
Elsie M  pl
Wilber A  pl
Harold E  pl
Helen L  pl
Orlando L
Newton, L L  far
Adriana (Austin  ho
Neda (m Dillingham  ho
*Geo L  trader
    Wayland, Mass
Addison E  far
*Effa A (m Warren
    E B'kfld

## O

Oldham, Benj F  far  Can 1
Sarah J (Irish  ho
*Simeon L  far  Caribou
*Anna F (m Proctor
    Waterbury, Conn
*Sam'l  mach
23 Farm, Waterbury, Conn
Alonzo I  far

## P

Palmer, Jos F  far  E Sum
Lizzie E (Cary  ho
Harry C  pl
Palmer, F W  sta agt  E Sum
Sadie D (Bonney  ho

*Howard S    trav auditor
            Portland

Bessie E             pl
Raymond H         pl
Elsie M              pl
Dorothy           / pl
Hazel               pl
Parsons, Emery   far    Can 1
Abbie A (Mitchell      ho
Edith M          nurse
*Addie L (m Gates
ho & nurse   Waterbury, Vt
Harold E           far
Dwight L           pl
Pearle, Wm    far    B'kfld
Poland, Almond   far    Can 1
Poland, Ada L (Rich     Sum
Wesley E           far
Walter P           far
Leon L             pl
Potter, T A    far    Can 1
Purkis, Amos L   far    B'kfld
*Walter H    far    E Turn
*Amos L Jr   far    B'kfld 2
*Alice M (m Parlin
       ′      Brownville
*Mattie C (m Hutchinson
               B'kfld
Purkis, A L    far    B'kfld
Nellie A (Allen       ho
Allen A           pl

## R

Records, Geo H        far
Lucy F (Jordan       ho
Glenis E
Records, L C   far    No Tur
Mary L (Jackson
*Harry A           car
585 Crescent, Brockton, Mass
*Newell P   blk    No Tur
Emma V           ho
Annie M           ho
Richard, Dolphus   far    Can
Mary (———        ho
Mary A
Ricker, M C    far    B'kfld
H Emily (Keene      ho
*Roscoe G   far    Tur Ctr
*Loura K (m Murch
             Mill, B'kfld
*Carroll H      med stu
   491 Mass Ave, Boston
Lester        stu & far
Ricker, Geo W   far    E Sum
Mary E (Cary         ho
Ripley, H F   far & blk   E Sum
Manda (Robinson     ho
Robinson, W S    mining eng
Harriet A (Fogg       ho
Winnifred M
          mineral Expert
Robinson, E A    far    E Sum 1
Charlotte L (Cloudman
Earl C           pl

Robinson, J O      far      Can 1
   Mary A (Carey              ho
   Theda A (m York            ho
Russell, A   far & sawyer   Can
   Florence M (Frye           ho
Russell, Ernest L    lab    Can
   Bessie M (Robertson        ho
   Geneva A
   Henry L
Russell, Wallace E   far   Can 1
   Hattie E (Staples          ho
   Maud E (m Barrill        B'kfld
   Ina M                      tr
   Amy I                      stu
Russell, Ada L (Pollard     Sum
Russell, Walter A     far & blk
                 E Sum 1
   Gertrude E (Beckler        ho
   Guy V                      pl
Russell, Mary A (Young     Sum
   *Martha E (m Poland
           Mechanic Falls
   Chas C                    far
Russell, Chas C     far     Sum
   Mary A Barrett             ho
   Chas B                     pl
Ryerson, Berdena B (Fletcher
                Can 1
   Castella B
Ryerson, Thos E             far
             E Sum 1
   Ruby W (Ford               ho
   *Frank L     car     Dixfield
   *Chas C B    mfg        Bret

Russell, Martha H
    (Butterfield     B'kfld
   *Geo W       lab      Turner
   *Chas O                   far
           Mechanic Falls
   *A L       diver      Boston
   *Dan'l F                   lab
           Wentworth, N H
   *Jno H   lab Mechanic Fls
   *Frank D  lab Chases Mls
   *Manevery (m Perry
             No Auburn
   *Susan D (m Mitchell
           Wentworth, N H
   *Jennie V (m Pratt
            Welchville
   Mary E (m High             ho

## S

Salone, A E              lumber
   Mrs Arthur——
Sampson, Mary A (Cobb
                Can 1
   *Alla M (m Allen
             No Wayne
   Herbert M      far      Can
   Lucy A (m Barker           ho
   Elisha T                   far
Sampson, E T     far     Can 1
   Edith I (Glover            ho
   Ida T
Sampson, H M   far   E Sum 1
   Gertie C (Alley            ho

Mildred V     pl
Kenneth E     pl
Sampson, Sarah (Walker
    Can 1
Martha A (m Marston ho
*Albert S    far    Weld
*Arthur E     s s op
    21 Pearl, Auburn
Sargent, Frances    far & blk
    Can 1
——(Lucas     ho
*——(m Dunn
    Keene's Mills
Martha     ho
Shaw, Addison J   far   B'kfld
*Vestie E (m McConnell
    Philadelphia, Pa
Helen May
S Nettie     ho
Margie     ho
Spaulding, Geo D    Can 1
Bertha A (Canwell    ho
James A     pl
Angie M     pl
Hazel F     pl
Geo A  ·   pl
Albert W
Susie M
Stetson, L C    far    Can 1
Martha F (Alley    ho
*Elisha L   bank cl   R Falls
Floyd A     lab
Ethel M     tr
Ralph L     pl

Stetson, T B W     Can 1
    far, town cl and tr
Nettie M (Keene    ho
Clarence E    stu & tr
Fred T     stu
Samuel N     far
M W     pl

**T**

Tinkham, E W     far
Tinkham, D G     far
Thomas, Nath   far   Can 1
*Humbert C far   West Sum
*Walter H     car
    Brockton, Mass
*Almira (m Bradford
    W Minot
*Nedella C (m Godfrey
    Brockton, Mass
Hattie L (Crockett    ho
Thomas, Tina M (Ryerson
    E Sum 1
Thompson, Martha A
    (Records    E Sum
Thompson, Harvey A    far
Cora M (Jordan
Thompson, Jno E far   E Sum
Margaret B (Bosworth ho
Thompson, Jno   far    Can 1
*Dora M (m Fuller    ho
Grace E (m Mitchell    ho
Thompson, Lumira    Can 1
Thompson, Angelia S
    (Hutchins    Can 1

Chas W      far
Carroll      carriage mkr
*Willie D    eng   E Dixfield
Flora M (m Patterson
Thurlow, I E      cream col
     Tur Ctr
   Mattie W (m Decoster   ho
Thurlow, J V    far    B'kfld 2
   Ella M (Holland
   Nellie A (m Gammon     ho
   Clinton S      pl
   Marion W      pl
Tucker, Wm E      R R Ser
   Edith M (Harris      ho
   Harold E
   Hazel
   Harris W
Thorn, Julia F (Farrar     ho
   Edwin E      lab
   Effie R (m Davenport    ho
   *Georgia (m Bucknam   ho
   Ira      lab     W Sum
Turner, O E far & Blk E Sum 1
   Bertie H (Glover      ho
Turner, E W     far    No Tur
   Inez L (Merrill      ho
   *Julius H   mill op   Dixfield
   Julia H (m Berry      ho
   Leon E      lab
Tyler, Jno F     far     Can 1
   Viola A (Parsons      ho
   Clara S (m Mendall     ho
   *Lettie M (m Bonney   Can
   John A      far
   Arthur N      pl

   Marion C      pl
Tyler, E S     far    E Sum 1
Warren, F L     far & gr dlr
     E Sum
   Lonella J (Hersey      ho
   Mary A      stu
   Percey      pl
   Geo L      pl
   Henry F      pl
Washburn, N B (Jones    Tur
   Gladys M      pl
Wells, Geo     lab    B'flkd 2
Whitman, Harriet M (Merrill
Williams, Florence F   ho & pl
Williams, Dora L   tr   No Tur
Wood, Geo V     far    B'kfld 2
   Mabel S (Gammon     ho
   M Methel
Woodman, Mary (Grant
     E Sum 1
   *Albin F     lumber & car
     Freeport
Woodman, S B   far   E Sum 1
   *Keith S      pack'g ho
     Boston, Mass
   Minnie H (Bosworth    ho

### Y

York, James E     far     Can 1
   Keziah F (Sanborn     ho
   *Clarence S   dlr   Augusta
   *Elmer H    blindman   Can
   *Ernest L   s s op   Wilton
Young, Geo     far     Can 1
Young, Lucy (Russell E Sum 1
   *L—— (m Newell E Sum 1
   *Frances E (m Poland
     E Sum 1
   Moses     far    E Sum 1
Young, Chas H   lab   E Sum 1